Furness

Furness Abbey

ROMANCE, SCHOLARSHIP
AND CULTURE

Christine Dade-Robertson

Centre for North-West Regional Studies
University of Lancaster
2000
Series Editor: Jean Turnbull

Furness Abbey: Romance, Scholarship and Culture

This volume is no. 42 in a series published by the
Centre for North-West Regional Studies at the University of Lancaster

Text copyright © Christine Dade-Robertson

First published in 2000 by
Centre for North-West Regional Studies
University of Lancaster

Designed and typeset in Adobe Garamond
by Carnegie Publishing, Carnegie House,
Chatsworth Road, Lancaster, LA1 4SL

Printed and bound in the UK by
Redwood Books, Trowbridge, Wilts

British Library Cataloguing-in-Publication Data
A CIP catalogue record for this book is available at the British Library

ISBN 1-86220-095-5

All rights reserved.
No part of this publication may be reproduced, stored in a retrieval
system, or transmitted in any form or by any means mechanical,
electronic, photocopying, recording or otherwise, without the prior
permission of the publisher.

for my parents
CHARLES and JUNE RACKHAM
with love and gratitude

The publishers gratefully acknowledge grants towards this publication from the Cumberland and Westmorland Antiquarian and Archaeological Society's Edmund Hodge Fund for Ecclesiastical Research and the Kirby Archives Trust.

Contents

Illustrations

Figures

Plates *(between pages 50 and 51)*

Foreword

> I have made a miserable botch of this description; it is no description, but merely an attempt to preserve something of the impression it made on me, and in this I do not seem to have succeeded at all.
>
> [Nathanial Hawthorne][1]

This remark, taken from one of the more obscure references to an interpretation of Furness Abbey, provides a revealing context for the present work. It was written by the American, Nathaniel Hawthorne during his visit to the site in July 1855. At this time the abbey was well on the way to becoming a popular tourist attraction. A railway station and hotel had recently been opened and guidebooks to the abbey were available for the first time. However, as Hawthorne readily admits, it was still virtually impossible to describe and understand the ruins in any meaningful way.

In some respects 1855 was a pivotal date in the history of the site's interpretation. This effectively began in the 1770s with the work of Thomas West, credited with producing the earliest known plan of the abbey, and continued uninterrupted until the completion in the 1930s of the major programme of restoration works set in motion by Sir Charles Peers. During this 160-year period, Furness Abbey witnessed a veritable 'Who's Who' of Georgian and Victorian writers, scholars, artists and photographers, each of whom sought to convey through their works the unique experience which the abbey engendered.

At the end of the eighteenth century, the picturesque and romantic qualities of the ruins were praised in the writings, among others, of William Gilpin and the Gothic novelist Ann (Mrs) Radcliffe, and illustrated by the likes of Thomas Hearne and the young J. M. W. Turner. Several important drawings, engravings and watercolours belong to the early nineteenth century, including those by William Green, William Close, Theodore Fielding, John Buckler and his son, and Robert Carlyle. Also at this time, the abbey featured in the works of William Wordsworth, who as a young man had a close affinity with the site.

The construction of the railway coincided with the first antiquarian excavations on the site by Thomas Beck and the abbey's appearance in specialist works on Cistercian architecture, most notably those of the Lancaster-based architect and medievalist Edmund Sharpe. From as early as 1856, the ruins were the subject of pioneering photography by Roger Fenton and later Francis Frith. The abbey also appeared in the writings of John Ruskin who often mentioned the beauty of 'my own sweet Furness' and the fact that it was being spoiled by the railway. By the turn of the century Sir William St John Hope had published the first systematic excavations and archaeological assessment of the site, paving the way to the placing of the ruins in the guardianship of the Office of Works, under Sir Charles Peers.

Furness Abbey has been a roofless ruin for over 460 years: that is about 50 years longer than it was a monastery! Its special interest for us now is rooted in the site's later history and interpretation, as well as the abbey's medieval and immediate post-Dissolution history. It is particularly appropriate and rewarding therefore that this book, by Christine Dade-Robertson, concentrates on this fascinating period when Furness became a focus for romantic excursion, antiquarian study and popular tourism. Drawing on the interpretations of numerous contemporary writers and artists, the book assesses the diverse ways in which the ruins have been exploited for their aesthetic qualities, as a spiritual place and as part of the expanding heritage industry of today. Based on a recent Lancaster University M.A. dissertation (which received a high distinction), Christine's work is both well researched and well written and introduces a number of fresh ideas. Enjoy the book and learn from it.

Finally, it is entirely fitting that Lancaster University, through its Centre for North-West Regional Studies, has published this important study. The University has had a long association with Furness Abbey, especially through its involvement with the Furness Abbey Survey Project. This project represented a major undertaking by the University's Archaeological Unit from 1985 to 1993, and periodically thereafter. As well as producing detailed record drawings, it was considered that research into available historical and documentary sources, both written and pictorial, would provide essential corroborative information which, analysed together with the field survey data, would lead to a greater understanding of the complicated chronology of the abbey buildings and their previous repairs. Apart from assisting the planned programme of conservation, this fuller knowledge of the site's development would equally lead to more informed presentation and marketing of the site to the visiting public. Thus, in its own way, the Furness Abbey Survey Project has added another layer to the long history of the site's interpretation. However, delighted though I am to be contributing this Foreword, and to find my own work figuring in the pages that follow, it is still a concern that the necessary resources have yet to be found to complete the project and publish the results in full.

Happily, the story does not end there. A new project is now being promoted at the site, based in the southern half of the precinct. Led by Community Action Furness and using European grant aid, the project aims to recapture local community and tourist interest in the abbey and its hinterland by creating a monastic garden as the starting-point for interpretation of the heritage of the surrounding landscape, complementing English Heritage's presentation of the abbey itself. Let us hope that this renewed interest in one of the finest monastic sites in the country, so often a surprise and delight to the modern day visitor, will extend the interpretation of Furness Abbey well into the new millennium.

JASON WOOD

Notes

1. Hawthorne, N., 'Our Old Home, and English Notebooks', p.2, in *The Complete Works of Nathaniel Hawthorne,* vol. VIII, with introductory notes by G. P. Lathrop (London, 1883).

Preface

> Experiments of multivocality in history that attempt to embody multiple perspectives as the very framework of their discourse are few because they so challenge the normal historical paradigm on an ultimately single authorial viewpoint. If the text is not to be a collection of quotations or a book of documentary sources, what can it be?
>
> [R. F. Berkhofer]

This work does not claim to represent a totally holistic view of the interpretations of a monastic site. It does propose, however, that the history of monastic sites did not cease once they became ruins after the Dissolution, but that their history continues. The 'multiple perspectives' on a monastic site are part of that history and are as valid to the historian as the physical remains and the medieval documentary evidence.

Following an introductory first chapter, three perspectives have been chosen to illustrate this. Chapter Two examines how the artists and writers of the Picturesque and Romantic Movement of the eighteenth and nineteenth centuries viewed the monastic ruin. Chapter Three explores the scholarly approach to such sites, perhaps perceived as the traditional approach. Finally, the fourth chapter focuses on the way that ruins have become part of the 'Heritage Industry', and how this has helped to preserve them and bring them into the public view. This, in turn, has created a multitude of popular and personal interpretations.

Furness Abbey has been chosen as a case study because, in the past, it has been well documented by historians as an important monastic site and it was, at the time of the Dissolution, the second wealthiest monastic Cistercian site in England after Fountains in Yorkshire. Its architectural detail does not compare with the splendour of some of the better known sites and this, coupled with its relative inaccessibility, helps account for its previous unpopularity when compared with other monastic ruins in the north. However, these substantial remains have inspired many of those who have discovered them and the abbey has now become a recognised part of the heritage circuit.

This book does not pretend to be an exhaustive study. It is based on the material which is commonly available to any person interested in

Furness Abbey. The work does not exclusively assess the interpretation of the ruin as a medieval monastic site but also argues that there are other interpretations of the site that were, and still are, targeted at the ruin in its own right rather than as a reflection of the past. The plural usages and interpretations discussed are common to every monastic site that boasts above-ground structural remains.

Berkhofer claims that to study these various representations may result in a text that is little more than 'a collection of quotations or a book of documentary sources'. This book includes an extensive number of quotations and a plethora of images which, it is argued, are essential to furthering our understanding of how the site has been interpreted. They are, of themselves, as valid a form of visual and documentary evidence as the ruin itself. In answer to Berkhofer's question, they can become integral to the argument and they therefore form an essential component of the text.

This book depends upon close integration of narrative and image and I am therefore extremely grateful to the following organisations and individuals for permitting us to use images in this book: Alice Leach; The Archaeological Journal; The Ashmolean Museum; Barrow Reference Library; The Cumberland and Westmorland Antiquarian and Archaeological Society (CWAAS); English Heritage; Jason Wood; The Royal Archaeological Institute; The Sankey Collection; The Society of Antiquaries and The Tate Gallery.

The original text formed part of the author's submission for a Master of Arts degree in Historical Research at Lancaster University. I would like to express my appreciation of the invaluable support provided to me by my supervisor, Dr Stephen Constantine, who gave unstintingly of his time. I would also like to acknowledge the contributions made by Dr David Shotter and Dr Keith Stringer of Lancaster University; Jason Wood who appreciates and understands Furness Abbey better than anyone else and who showed such an interest in my research; the staff of English Heritage particularly John Moore and Tom Burrows; the staff at Lancaster University Library, the Ruskin Library, the Harris Reference Library, Preston, the Lancashire and Cumbria Record Offices, and Barrow Local History Library; Dr Richard Newman of the Archaeology Department, Lancaster University; and Mrs Alison Grant for help with the preparation of the text. Last, but not least, a special thank you to my family who have supported me throughout my studies, particularly my husband, Steven, and my son, Martyn, who have contributed both photographic and computer skills.

Notes

1. R. F. Berkhofer, 'A point of view on viewpoints in historical practice', in F. Ankersmit and H. Kellner (eds), *A New Philosophy of History* (London, 1995), p. 190.

CHAPTER ONE

Introduction

> Ruins signal simultaneously an absence and a presence; they show, they *are*, an intersection of the visible and the invisible. Fragmented, decayed structures, which no longer serve their original purpose, point to an absence – a lost, invisible whole. But their visible presence also points to durability, even if that which *is* is no longer what it once was.
>
> [Salvator Settis] [1]

Buildings that become ruins, as the above quotation suggests, no longer function in the way their originators had intended, yet they still have the power to influence thought. Manifested in poetry and literature, academic theses, drawings, paintings, photographs or in pursuits of enjoyment and contemplation, the interpretation of ruins is a fascinating subject matter in its own right.

The quotation was taken from a book written as a companion volume to an exhibition which was staged by the Getty Research Institute from December 1997 to February 1998. The collection, a combination of visual evidence in the form of artefacts, paintings and photographs juxtaposed with text, was selected to investigate the reasons why ruins promote 'curiosity, *frisson*, reverence and pleasure', [2] and how ruins themselves have ultimately been interpreted. Michael Roth argues that, in order to understand the exhibition, the visitor must first understand the nature of ruins that are 'emblematic of transience and persistence over time'. [3] They can also be appreciated as much for what is absent as for that which is still present.

Ruins change over time due to the onset of decay generated by nature or man. Because a ruin is constantly decaying there is a risk that it will be permanently lost. The paradox is that it is the decaying process that promotes a desire to protect and even reconstruct, thus altering or breaking the progression of decline. Whether the emphasis has been on the ruin as historically important, as a building that needs to be examined and understood as part of the past, or on the ruin as a pleasing image which excites the imagination, the last hundred years has witnessed a surge of interest in protecting such sites.

In previous centuries, nature was allowed to take its course and the ravages of time added an aesthetic quality which became part of the attraction of the ruin. Ruins were celebrated, not lamented, and there was little desire to halt the inevitable deterioration. However, all known ruins have been, in some way, reclaimed. Nature reclaims the ruin by gradually taking back what has once been taken from her, whereas man, as the creator of the original building, reclaims it as part of his heritage and may 'freeze' the ruin at a moment in time through poetry, paintings or photography.

Similarly, Gill Chitty argues that 'intervention to maintain a ruin seeks to freeze it "with all the evidences" at the particular and arbitrary moment in time when the decision to preserve it has been taken'.[4] Modern thinking in the UK on the preservation of ruins tends to concentrate on arresting any further decay rather than replacing what has already been lost. It could be argued that a ruin belongs to the past, and cannot become part of the present unless it is fully restored, but then it ceases to be a ruin. John Ruskin believed that any kind of restoration of a ruin destroys the ruin itself. He wrote at length on the subject in the nineteenth century and was incensed when the ruins of Europe, which he loved so much, were being 'restored' to their previous grandeur.[5]

This debate over the appropriate level of intervention is reflected in the records of the many architectural and archaeological societies and journals of the mid-nineteenth century. Various levels of restoration were defined and this led to sites being categorised as 'living' or 'dead'. A dead site was viewed as one which was preserved as evidence of the past. In 1913 Sir Charles Peers wrote:

> There is a great distinction between buildings which are still occupied and buildings which are in ruins. Buildings which are in use are still adding to their history; they are alive. Buildings which are in ruin are dead; their history is ended. There is all the difference in the world in their treatment.[6]

A ruin is, however, part of the present, just because it exists. The ruin itself, therefore, continues to live. It may alter through time; in fact it cannot fail to do so, but the changes are just part of its history. Once a ruin becomes visible, in the sense that it attracts interest, the changing process does not cease. How the ruin's future history evolves, however, depends largely on the type of interest it has attracted. The observer will 'invent' the ruin from his own perspective.

The Getty Research Institute used the potency of the image and the strength of the written word to illustrate how ruins have been invented and reconstructed. These same media will be employed in this book to aid our understanding of the many ways in which people have invented, viewed, and been influenced by ruins in England. Tangible remains provide greater immediacy than a written book or article, and the images of the remains discussed in this book provide a valuable source of information. However the images, like the ruins, are themselves mute and therefore an analysis of the associated text will be used as a means of promoting our understanding of them. Similarly the written documents which are referred to here will be analysed and used to further our understanding of the ruin in the context of the time in which they were written. It is to be hoped that these images and quotations will work well together and will aid the reader's understanding and experience of a monastic site.

Some of the most significant ruins to be found in this country are of ecclesiastical origin. The wholesale destruction of monasteries during the first third of the sixteenth century created an extensive legacy of monastic ruins for future generations. However, the religious climate of the decades immediately after the Dissolution of the Monasteries almost removed the ruins from public view. Although revered and lamented by some, they tended to be identified with Popish associations which, at the time, were viewed with suspicion. Thus they were seen, not as something to be recreated or rescued, but as something to be plundered, ignored and forgotten. However, over time, these monastic institutions, so important a part of everyday life and supported by all levels of society during the Middle Ages, gradually assumed a 'foreign' quality which fostered a more detached interest, devoid of the previous emotions which their existence as unmutilated religious institutions and their violent destruction had produced. The ruin now generated a mixture of curiosity and sympathy. This interest has continued and has taken many forms since Sir William Dugdale wrote his *Monasticon Anglicanum* in the third quarter of the seventeenth century, providing, for the first time, a published collection of monastic records. This brought monasticism back on to the agenda of public interest.

To tackle a study that encompasses all the monastic ruins in England, and how their remains have been viewed, would be beyond the scope of this work. An overview of the interpretation of monastic ruins will, therefore, be attempted using one particular ruin as a case study.

An often neglected, yet imposing example of a monastic ruin, large parts of which survive above ground today, is that of Furness Abbey in Cumbria. The history of the Abbey of St Mary in Furness began when a future king of England, Stephen, Count of Boulogne, granted some land at Tulketh, near Preston, Lancashire, to the Benedictine Savignac order in 1123. However, it would appear, the site was not considered to be suitable for the building of a monastery and therefore, according to the extant medieval documents, the monks moved, in 1127, to a more appropriate location, that of Furness in Lancashire North of the Sands. Twenty years later the community at Furness, together with all the daughter houses of the Savignac order in Europe, was swallowed up by a more powerful order of monks, the Cistercians.[7]

In common with the majority of monastic institutions in England during the reign of King Henry VIII, Furness Abbey was forcibly abandoned by its clerical inhabitants when the deed of surrender was signed by Roger Pyle, Abbot of Furness, on 9 April 1537. The Dissolution of the Monasteries created, over a period of a few years, hundreds of ruins. Many motives have been put forward for this unique event in the annals of English history but it is likely that it was a monarch's greed for material wealth and secular power over the Church which led to the destruction of the buildings at Furness and elsewhere, thus ensuring that they were never able to re-form. They were stripped of their valuables and, in particular, the lead from the roofs, leaving the fabric exposed to the elements.

Furness Abbey's history over the century or so following the Dissolution mirrors the history of other monastic institutions in that it was largely rejected as a place of interest other than as a quarry for building material. The abbey continued to decay due to the corrosive elements of the weather, the growth of vegetation and, as a survey of the surrounding area would confirm, the local propensity for using the dressed stones for domestic dwellings, walls and bridges.

Whilst the ruins of Furness Abbey tell us much about its monastic historical past, the site's history continued after the Dissolution. This book will assess the diverse ways in which the ruin has been exploited for its aesthetic qualities, as a spiritual place, and as part of the expanding heritage industry right up to the present day.

Furness Abbey provides a particularly good example because the original site, during its period as a working monastery, was filled with an impressive array of architecture, some of which has survived into this century. English Heritage, today's guardian of the site, describes such ruins as 'important documents of both Christianity and Medieval life, as well as being picturesque landmarks'.[8]

A wide range of sources will be used, representing work from many disciplines. These will include photographs; paintings and engravings; poems; fiction; newspapers; local guidebooks and official guides to the site; printed local histories of various dates; national history books; and archaeological, architectural and tourist literature, including site plans and maps. Many of these will be used as both primary and secondary sources in that they reveal as much about the writers and artists and the time in which they lived as about the monastic site itself.

For example when Thomas West, writing in 1774, tells us that 'In magnitude, this abbey was the second in England belonging to the Cistercian monks, and the next in opulence after Fountains abbey in Yorkshire',[9] he is informing us about the history of the site as understood from a survey of the original documents detailing the revenues of the abbey as compared with other monastic houses. In this sense, West can be used as a secondary source. However, when West describes the condition of two tombstones, which were found within the abbey precincts he says:

> They bear the marks of the ignorant zeal of some bigoted leveller, whose passion was to erase the memory of every thing that bore the appearance of distinction, and who strove to reduce all things into one mass of confusion. [10]

In saying this he is making a value judgement at the time of writing, therefore telling the modern reader more about his own, and perhaps his contemporaries', interpretation of the site.

Writing in 1995, Professor Bann described a wash drawing, shown in Figure 1, executed by Ernest Dainville, *c.*1850, of the thirteenth-century Eglise Toussaint, in Angers. This church has since been restored but in the 1850s, when this sketch was made, it was a ruin. Bann says:

> They were talking to each other, the two gentlemen in top hats and frockcoats, who stand in the centre of the aisle of the ruined church. One of them, evidently the person who knows the site and its attractions, has his left arm outstretched in a generous gesture of reference: his companion, who is obviously a visitor being harangued, stands responsively with his face directed towards the objects indicated by his mentor. Close by, there is a third visitor, just as formally dressed but without the top hat, who balances a sketching block on his knees: he looks past his companions in the direction of the other side of the aisle, where a number of other sculptural objects are clearly on display. [11]

Bann argues that the wash drawing is of a 'scene for instruction, as well as for reverie', [12] and this is a theme that will be developed in this book. Taking the metaphor further, the first gentleman in a top hat will become the antiquarian or 'expert' who studies the ruin for the purposes of learning about the past. His companion will become the tourist who views the ruin without the depth of knowledge possessed by his friend, but with equal fascination and enjoyment. The man who sketches will become the person who views the ruin for its aesthetic value. The main text is therefore divided into three chapters under the general headings: 'The Picturesque and the Romantic', 'The Scholarly Challenge: Antiquarians, Archaeologists and Historians', and 'Tourists and the Heritage Industry'. These three sections allow for a comprehensive examination of the various ways in which Furness Abbey has been interpreted since the eighteenth century, although all three interrelate chronologically and overlap in their content.

Chapter Two will explore how the ruins were reclaimed by those interested in their aesthetic qualities. In 1757, Edmund Burke published *A Philosophical Enquiry into the Origin of our Ideas of the Sublime and the*

Beautiful which looked at objects in terms of how they promoted emotions. Brian Bailey argues that this concept was 'a psychological rather than an objective approach, emphasising spiritual values and emotions instead of the universal virtues of flawless form and symmetry which had long been taken almost as absolute truths'.[13] The interest that was generated by this work feeds directly into the emergence of the 'Romantic Movement'. We can trace the Romantic movement from the middle of the eighteenth century and, although the passions that ruins conjured up, and still have the power to conjure up today, are complex and difficult to define, the strong elements of imagination and individual expression, the emotions which encompassed fear, desolation, and love, are central in our understanding of this period in history. The decay, splendour and picturesque qualities of ruins provided a focus for the Romantic movement.

The Romantic era covered a period of approximately one hundred years, although some would argue that it survived into the twentieth century in the form of Expressionism and Neo-Expressionism. It produced many artistic and literary figures and the ruin, especially the monastic ruin, was often the vehicle for their creations. The accent was on nature reclaiming the ruins: the ivy clad walls and air of abandonment were crucial elements of the picturesque. Religious ideology or a concern to arrest the decaying process did not encumber this view. The observer was aware that the past could not be brought back to life, but nature could restore the balance by reclaiming the ruins.

Whilst on a visit to Tintern Abbey, William Gilpin, a 1770s traveller wrote: 'A ruin is a sacred thing. Rooted for ages in the soil; assimilated to it; and becoming, as it were, part of it; we consider it as a work of nature, rather than of art.'[14] Arthur Young, another writer of the same period wrote, after a visit to Fountains Abbey: 'We generally find them in retired, neglected spots, half-filled with rubbish, and the habitation rather of bats, owls and wild beasts, than of man.'[15] Both these early writers approved of the abbeys' neglected state in that they did not write of any regret for the condition of the buildings.

The 'Picturesque Movement', in sympathy with the earlier travellers cited above, produced images of the ruin in 'an anti-nostalgic or even anti-antiquarian mode of relating to ruins'.[16] These images were not meant to represent a 'true' impression of the buildings, but rather one that produced certain responses in the beholder.

The Lake District, including Lancashire North of the Sands in which Furness Abbey is located, had a key role to play in the Picturesque and Romantic movement. Chapter Two will therefore focus on how Furness Abbey was viewed by the writers, artists and poets of the Romantic period.

Overlapping chronologically, and associated with a revived interest in ruins, there emerged a preoccupation with monastic remains as visual

Ernest Dainville, Ancien Eglise Toussaint, *c.* 1850, wash drawing. [Figure 1]

documents of the past. In Chapter Three the roles of the antiquarian, the archaeologist, the historian and the architect will be analysed as representing another interpretation of the monastic ruin. Here the emphasis is on preservation and the study of the existing architecture for what it can tell us of the medieval past. In order to understand this past, it is argued, the physical remains can be used as historical evidence, in conjunction with the contemporary extant manuscripts.

The early antiquarians were elitist in that they wrote of their findings in a way that was not easily accessible to others who did not share their knowledge. The historian, on the other hand, emerging in the nineteenth century, first in the universities and then locally, has been responsible for making it possible for any interested party to share in the view of the ruin as a 'passport to the past'. The archaeologists provided complementary evidence which, as the twentieth century has progressed, has improved with technology.

By the late eighteenth century, architectural historians were publishing papers and books accompanied by good quality and detailed architectural drawings of the buildings. Architects like John Britton, who published his *Architectural Antiquities* (1807–26) and *Cathedral Antiquities* (1814–35), fostered an interest in medieval architecture, and these publications served as records of the architecture of many ruins which have since been lost. As the nineteenth century progressed, the cult of 'Gothic' architecture filtered into modern designs that tried to reproduce the work of the medieval masons.

The clearing of the site of rubble and vegetation in order to gain access to the 'skeleton' did nothing to enhance the Picturesque view of the site, but was a crucial element in the preservation and understanding of the ruin as a former monastic community. It was not, however, until nearly the end of the nineteenth century that excavations of monastic sites were attempted. At Furness Abbey, eminent scholars Sir William St John Hope, Sir Harold Brakspear and Sir Charles Peers, over a period of several decades, investigated the ruins and helped to reconstruct the ground plan of the abbey.

The first ground plan of Furness Abbey was produced by Thomas West in 1770 and was published in his *The Antiquities of Furness* in 1774. From then on archaeologists and historians produced increasingly complicated plans that often incorporated an estimated chronology of the construction of the buildings by the use of shading and colouring. An analysis of the plans of Furness Abbey from 1774 until the latest plan of 1998 will be incorporated into Chapter Three. Not only do the plans give an indication of newer findings over the last two centuries, as more of the remains have been uncovered or identified, but they also give an insight into which parts of the site most interested the author of a particular plan. These plans are also evidence of the advance of new technology and a growing knowledge of monastic institutions through the study of similar sites in Britain and Europe.

The development of scholarly interest in the site, and concern for the possible destruction and eventual loss of the structural remains of the ruins, created a sense of responsibility for the conservation of what was left. This was initially the concern of the private owner of the site but, with the introduction of legislation drafted to protect ancient monuments through government agencies, this became a public issue. Furness Abbey was privately owned by the Cavendish family during the nineteenth century, and many members of this family took an interest in the site. An attempt was made to clear some of the rubble, and local histories were encouraged. When the Office of Works took the site into State care in 1923, they provided official guidebooks to disseminate knowledge to a wider audience. The focus of the 'tidied up' site was on the ruin as a place for education rather than something of beauty. By 1983 the site was in the guardianship of English Heritage and, although the emphasis was still on the preservation of the remains, there was also an attempt to foster public interest in the buildings as a historical document.

Whereas Romanticism influenced attitudes towards the role of ruins in the landscape, and the academics concentrated on the interpretation of the ruins as visual evidence of a lost past, the advent of tourism created an altogether more complicated interpretation of monastic ruins. Associated with the rise of mass tourism in the twentieth century was the creation of the 'Heritage Industry', the subject of Chapter Four.

The early traveller to the Lake District was usually searching for the picturesque. Burke's 'sublime and beautiful' was now being interpreted as a form which could be framed as in a picture. The 'collectors' of the picturesque were beginning to plan tours in their pursuit of romantic and picturesque landscapes. Norman Nicholson tells us that 'After 1790, the tourists were no longer pioneers or explorers; they were holiday makers.'[17] Roads were improved to aid the tourist, but it was the arrival of the railway in the 1840s that really opened up the Lake District.

Chapter Four will examine the local guidebooks to the Furness site and the surrounding area. There are many of these early tourist guides for the Lake District, and they often contain some reference to Furness Abbey as an attraction for the visitor. The older works are often difficult to read, mainly being produced by the antiquarian whose emphasis was on the scholastic. However, as tourism became less elitist and the middle and working classes began to discover the pleasures of travel, the guidebooks became less academic and more descriptive, focusing on individual observation. For example, in 1835, the celebrated poet long associated with the Lake District, William Wordsworth, produced *A Guide Through the District of the Lakes*. Tourists were soon able to purchase maps, postcards and souvenirs of their travels and were bombarded with advertisements in books, on billboards and in newspapers, which extolled the virtues of the landscape.

As the awareness of the monastic site as an interesting place to visit developed, visitors were provided with explanatory pamphlets to aid their understanding. The earlier works varied in their layout and content, but eventually they became standardised, especially once the sites were taken into State care. The Ministry of Works' *Blue Guides* were rather bland and cheaply produced but, as the heritage industry began to be more concerned with the 'marketing' of the whole package, the guidebooks became glossier and were more often updated to reflect the latest information and the increasingly diverse interests of the reader.

In a way, the heritage industry reflects all three very complex interpretations of a ruin. Not only will visitors have their own personal interpretation of the site but the scholarly work resulting from the research of the antiquarian, archaeologist and historian contributes significantly to the displays and literature which visitors to the abbey can view and purchase at the sites today. Painters, poets and writers still visit abbeys to gain inspiration, and examples of their work, and that of their predecessors, are also included in the displays and guidebooks. Whatever the reason for the attraction of any monastic site, it is this interest which will ensure its survival for future generations.

Notes

1. Quote from S. Settis (Director, The Getty Research Institute for the History of Art and the Humanities), 'Foreword', in M. S. Roth, C. Lyons and C. Merewether, *Irresistible Decay: Ruins Reclaimed* (Los Angeles, 1997), p. vii.
2. Roth, Lyons and Merewether, *Irresistible Decay*, p. 1.
3. Ibid., p. xi.
4. G. Chitty, 'A prospect of ruins', *Trans. of the Association for Studies in the Conservation of Historic Buildings*, xii (1987), p. 43.
5. K. O. Garrigan, *Ruskin on Architecture: His Thought and Influence* (Wisconsin, 1973), p. 160.
6. C. Peers (1913), quoted in K. Emerick, 'Archaeology and architecture: a tradition of collaboration', *Journal of Architectural Conservation*, i (Mar. 1997), p. 59.
7. J. Bulmer (ed.), *History, Topography and Directory of Furness and Cartmel comprising its history and archaeology, physical and geological features with separate Historical and Topographical Description of each town, parish and manor* (2nd edn, Preston, 1911); F. Evans, *Furness and Furness Abbey, or A Companion through the Lancashire part of the Lake District* (Ulverston, 1842); and, for a fuller account of the history of Furness Abbey: T. A. Beck, *Annales Furnesienses: History and Antiquities of the Abbey of Furness* (London, 1844).
8. English Heritage, *Scheduled Monuments* (London, 1996).
9. T. West, *The Antiquities of Furness* (Ulverston, 1813), p. 71.
10. Ibid., p. 119.
11. S. Bann, 'History as competence and performance: notes on the Ironic Museum, in Ankersmit and Kellner, *New Philosophy of History*, p. 201.
12. Ibid., p. 203.
13. B. Bailey, *The National Trust Book of Ruins* (London, 1984).
14. W. Gilpin, *Observations on the Mountains and Lakes of Cumberland and Westmorland* (London, 1786; repr. Richmond, 1973). For more information on Tintern Abbey, see J. Knight, *Tintern Abbey and the Romantic Movement* (London, 1977).
15. A. Young, *A Six Months Tour through the North of England* (London, 1770).
16. Roth, Lyons and Merewether, *Irresistible Decay*, p. 7.
17. N. Nicholson, *The Lakers: The First Tourists* (London, 1972).

CHAPTER TWO

The Picturesque and the Romantic

> What has led the building upward is human will; what gives it its present appearance is the brute, downward-dragging, corroding, crumbling power of nature. Still, so long as we can speak of a ruin at all and not a mere heap of stones, this power does not sink the work of man into the formlessness of mere matter. There rises a new form, which, from the standpoint of nature, is entirely meaningful, comprehensible, differentiated. Nature has transformed the work of art into material for her own expression, as she had previously served as material for art.
>
> [Georg Simmel, 1858–1918] [1]

Georg Simmel, a German sociologist and philosopher, was renowned for his original thinking. The above quotation has been used here to provide a loose description of the complex movement, which has been termed the Picturesque and the Romantic. This in turn was a reflection of a wider movement based on the rejection of the political and social changes embodied in the philosophy of the French Enlightenment with its emphasis on reason and logic. R. W. Harris argues that 'David Hume pointed the way, Edmund Burke provided the philosophical accompaniment and Sir Walter Scott provided the romantic nostalgia.' [2] From about 1780 there was a movement towards nature and a search for a non-rational explanation for human behaviour, often coupled with a renewed sense of history.

Simmel identifies the ruin in the landscape as a product of the art of nature. Nature has reclaimed the ruins although, as he observes, the process is not yet complete; it is not yet a 'heap of stones'; it can still be identified as a man-made structure. This was the attraction of the ruin in the landscape that was, literally, framed by artists and celebrated, romanticised or lamented by writers during the eighteenth and nineteenth centuries. This chapter will explore this development, particularly in relation to images of Furness Abbey, both visual and written. It will be argued that the picturesque representations of the abbey, whilst they complemented the views of both contemporary scholars and tourists, produced enduring images which have a unique value of their own.

John Smith, Furness Abbey i[n] Gilpin, *Observati[ons] on the Mountain[s] and Lakes,* 1786 [Figure 2]

A fascination for landscape scenes first developed during the educational and cultural Grand Tours of rich English gentlemen when Italian artists like Claude Lorraine (1600–82) and Salvator Rosa (1615–73) were studied and became popular. Lorraine often included a ruin in his paintings which otherwise tended to be calm and tranquil. Rosa's style was more chaotic but, alongside his precipices, chasms and torrents, he often added a ruined building, increasing the dramatic effect.[3] The result of studying their pictures was to induce travellers to measure real landscapes against the standard of beauty depicted by Lorraine and Rosa. As early as 1712, Joseph Addison wrote in *The Spectator*: 'We find the Works of Nature still more pleasant, in the more they resemble those of Art.'[4]

The Rev. William Gilpin (1724–1804), a travelling parson renowned for his travel literature, used the term 'picturesque' to include all subjects, especially landscapes, considered to be worthy of painting.[5] As the cult grew, so by the second half of the eighteenth century, the Englishman was travelling around his own country in search of picturesque images that he could paint or write about. He particularly sought out ruins as 'pleasing melancholy' and 'agreeable horror'.[6] The sparsely populated, untamed Lake District became a favourite place for those in search of the picturesque. William Gilpin visited the Lake District in the summer of 1772, and his subsequent writings were, according to Nicholson, 'the first picturesque survey of the district'. However, Nicholson also observed that, due to the short duration of his stay and the fact that he had no eye for detail, his view was very superficial.[7] Gilpin believed that the irregular shape of nature could not be improved. The ruin, too, was broken, having lost its original architectural perfection, and to Gilpin it was now more in keeping with the aesthetic qualities of nature, of which it was becoming a part. In fact when Gilpin visited Tintern Abbey he was moved to suggest that perhaps those parts of the abbey which were still whole might be improved by breaking them up with a mallet.[8] Moreover, Gilpin was appalled on a visit to Fountains Abbey in 1770, when he discovered that the ruins were in the process of being landscaped and tidied up. He commented on 'A legal right the proprietor unquestionably has to deform his ruin as he pleases', but it was a legal right he very obviously deplored.[9] Gilpin therefore approved of the monastic ruin which was neglected and left to decay.

Once found, the image was reproduced in visual or written form and captured in time. Enhanced by foliage and vegetation, a ruin was a fragmented thing: no longer a flawless form, perceived as being sublime, melancholy and at the same time picturesque in its decay. It was now part of the landscape, even perhaps an enhancement of the landscape. The emphasis was on nature reclaiming, and therefore the decaying process was an integral element in the picturesque view. Once captured on canvas or paper, however, as Roth says, 'natural decay is made part of an artistic project and stopped'.[10] Of course, in reality, the decaying process was not stopped. The importance of the ruin was not in its architecture, nor in its archaeological interest; in fact the historical importance of the building was not even considered. It was the ruins themselves, not what they had once been, which those seeking the picturesque and the romantic primarily focused on.

'urner, Furness .bbey, from his Northern Tour, 97. Reproduced y permission of e Tate Gallery. [Figure 3]

The romance of the monastic ruin was in its ability to stimulate so many emotions, often of a very personal and private nature. A ruined castle was often associated with noise, violence and terror, whereas a monastery was more often viewed as a place of contemplation and serenity. Cistercian monasteries in particular were built in remote and isolated places and, as ruins, in the days before mass tourism, were often viewed by visitors alone or in small groups. Frequently, they were seen as melancholy places that promoted the sensations of sadness and reflection, or even of a haunted place to be feared.

The spiritual essence of monastic ruins can be almost tangible, but the emphasis in the eighteenth century was on the secular, not the religious. Although there must have been, at that time, some who regretted the loss of the monasteries as spiritual centres, the prevalent religious climate of the time was illustrated by Sir Uredale Price (1747–1829) when in 1794 in his 'Essay on the Picturesque', he celebrated the ecclesiastical ruins by saying that 'we may glory that the abodes of tyranny and superstition are in ruin'.[11]

The nostalgia that the ruin sometimes evoked was more often related to the 'perceived' loss of the simplicity of life in the country than to the site as a charitable and sacred place. Many of the visitors would find it easy to contrast the secluded valley, as old as nature itself, with the hustle and grime of the modern industrial town. Moreover, the visitor might only be aware of the ruin as the neglected and quiet place it now appeared to be, and might find it impossible to imagine it as a busy and turbulent place. Ignored or forgotten were the acoustic properties of the massive church enhancing the singing of the monks, their voices raised to God in prayer, and the ringing of the bell to summon the brethren to their place of worship. Forgotten too were the sounds of the workmen as their tools struck the stone, as their saws sliced through the wood and their hammers knocked in the nails and posts as the buildings were erected and altered over the years.

The picturesque view is never crowded with people. Often the artist and the writer would add or refer to animals who quietly grazed, a peasant or two using the remains as shelter for his flock and an occasional visitor or small group of visitors, who had come to enjoy the solitude and appreciate the awe-inspiring majesty of the ruins, no longer a seat of power and authority, but now a place of private pleasure and contemplation.

It is important to note that the Picturesque movement produced art, poetry and literature, but that these were not intended to be used in any serious study of the monastic building and its history. However, these interpretations do add to the history of the site itself, and as such can be used as a primary source in respect of the time when they were created. Further, the ecclesiastical historian can use these interpretations as evidence of how the buildings might have looked at that time. These sources cannot be entirely relied upon to represent fact, however. The artist's and writer's impressions of the ruin were often not accurate. Artists would add animals, shadowy figures and would deliberately soften the stark shapes of the building. In addition, the perspective was often not faithfully reproduced. The view of the ruins would be seen through the imagination rather than the reality. Thompson observes that 'the ruin was there to stimulate and excite the onlooker; whatever increased the theatrical effect – ivy or moonlight – was desirable to heighten the sensation'.[12] It was the sensations that ruins generated which were important for the romantic and those seeking the picturesque, not the unsentimental and meticulous view of the scholar.

Two modern writers, reflecting on these sensibilities in the middle of the twentieth century, provide us with thought provoking and, in some

Photograph,
gure 4] Furness
Abbey, north
transept and
crossing from
outh transept.

Inset: Furness
bbey, painting
by Daniel
Crosthwaite,
engraved by
. W. Topham.
[Figure 5]

Turner, Tintern Abbey. Reproduced by permission of the Ashmolean Museum. [Figure 6]

ways, conflicting observations on both the Picturesque movement and the nature of ruins. Nicholson, in his critique of the picturesque, observes that this view was a 'complete distortion of perception', and 'The Picturesque reduces the world to a mere scribbling pad for man; it makes a convenience of nature.'[13] Rose Macaulay, on the other hand, believed that ruins should not be restored 'unless their use is necessary' because they are 'part of the aesthetic kingdom of the eye and mind; like the poetry and painting of desolation [and are] more romantic when they stand wholly ruinous among their old walls'.[14] She describes the 'picturesque' view of ruins as an observation of

> the impression they individually make, by their beauty, or their strangeness, or their shattered intimidations that strike so responsive a nerve in our destruction seeking souls. Or, more usually by their mere picturesqueness.[15]

What Macaulay is describing here is a disparate assortment of complex emotions, which were expressed through art, poetry and prose. Whatever one's personal view of ruins and their interpretation during this period, as Simmel says, a ruin 'from the standpoint of nature', provides a valid, albeit subjective view of the landscape.[16] The place of Furness Abbey in the Romantic and the Picturesque will now be explored in more detail through two interpretations: that of the artist, and that of the writer.

The artists of the eighteenth and nineteenth centuries were, some would argue, privileged to be able to view the abbey at its most picturesque. At this time it was still cloaked in ivy and moss which climbed up the walls and columns and around the windows and covered, like a carpet, the broken bits of rubble which lay in mounds on the floors of the buildings, and the whole view was framed by bushes and trees. Plate 8 reproduces a recent aerial photograph, sold as a postcard at the modern visitor centre, to illustrate the proximity of the modern town which has crept closer to the ruins over the last two centuries. Although the little valley is still secluded today, surrounded by trees and open pastureland, all the vegetation has been removed from the ruins and many of the trees that we see in the old drawings have disappeared. Much of the rubble has also been disposed of, and the grassy areas around the standing stones are, if not manicured, at least kept well trimmed. Malcolm Andrews observed, when writing about monastic ruins which have been 'rescued' as monuments of our heritage, that when they have been tidied up they possess 'more the air of an artificial ruin in a garden, than that of an ancient decayed Abbey'.[17]

Most would agree that the photographic image, seen in Plate 8 provides a 'truer' image of the ruin than a painting or drawing. However, the ruin is just as much 'framed' by this visual image as by that of the picturesque artist, and the photographer also has access to a range of techniques, such

T. Allom, Furne Abbey, *c.*1836. [Figure 7]

as the use of light and shadow, to enhance the image. Even a photograph will never therefore be a completely 'true' representation. This theme of 'truth' versus 'artistic interpretation' will be developed in the context of the picturesque style of drawing and painting.

Furness Abbey did not escape the cult of the picturesque. Gilpin visited Furness Abbey and, in 1786, when his *Observations on the Mountains and Lakes of Cumberland and Westmorland* was published, he wrote of the abbey that it had 'suffered, from the hand of time, only such depredations as picturesque beauty requires'.[18] Gilpin included, in this topographical work, a hazy and somewhat atmospheric aquatint of the infirmary chapel at Furness Abbey which is shown in Figure 2.[19]

One of the greatest landscape artists of the period during which the Picturesque and Romantic Movement was at its height was Joseph Mallord William Turner (1775–1851). His itinerary of a tour through the North of England in 1797, at the age of twenty-two, included Furness Abbey. Unfortunately Turner only made three sketches of the abbey, executed in pencil. One was of the gateway and old manor house, one was of the infirmary chapel from the east, and the third was of the north transept and crossing from the south transept. The latter is shown in Figure 3.[20] Sadly none of these three was ever, as far as we know, developed into a full painting.

Carlyle, 'Furness Abbey from the West'. [Figure 8]

What is evident from the sketch in Figure 3 is Turner's ability to create an extremely accurate representation of the building. If one were to stand in the same spot today, the same view would be observed. Although this is only a rough sketch, the detail is remarkably clear. Turner would have been sitting on the night stairs looking at the crossing of the church towards the great window of the north transept. Although this is not possible today, without the aid of a ladder, access to the night stairs in the south chapel was still possible in 1797, and a photograph, taken by Roger Fenton in 1856 and which can be seen on page 9 in English Heritage's guidebook of 1998, shows this clearly. A comparison of Turner's sketch and a modern photograph, shown in Figure 4, illustrates that Turner's sketches were based on what he actually saw.

Figure 5 is a painting by Daniel Crosthwaite, engraved by F. W. Topham *c.*1845, which is of the same view that Turner sketched, developed into a picturesque drawing in a similar style to that of Turner.[21] Figure 6 is a copy of a painting by Turner of a similar interior view of Tintern Abbey. These give us indications of how Turner may have 'improved' the Furness sketch, had he developed it further. Crosthwaite made use of figures and additional foliage whilst Turner, in his Tintern Abbey painting, adds mood and atmosphere by his use of light and the addition of picturesque elements. In this example Turner has added a figure, a

R. Carlyle.
Left: 'Furness Abbey from th East'. [Figure 9

Right: 'Furness Abbey, interior the Chapter House'. [Figure

great deal of foliage, and a fishing basket, carelessly abandoned in the foreground. Turner produced this painting in his studio and although his sketch, made on site, provided him with the bare bones of the architecture, it was his imagination that provided the 'picturesque' image we can see in the completed painting.[22] David Hill defines the purpose of Turner's art as an attempt to 'discover the mental truth of a site, as perceived by a living rather than mechanical imagination', and Turner's sketches are described as 'a model of intelligent engagement with visual experience'.[23] Turner took the literal view of the ruins he sketched and then later, using his creative ability, turned them into beautiful paintings enhanced by the addition of colour and objects that he saw only in his imagination.

This imaginative interpretation of views and buildings was to be copied and developed by other artists. An early example can be seen in Figure 7, a painting of Furness Abbey executed by the Victorian topographer Thomas Allom *c.*1836.[24] Allom was well known for his topographical prints of the northern counties of England in the period from 1825 to 1845. In this drawing, the abbey is barely recognisable as Furness. The architectural lines are not defined and much of the structure is deliberately buried under rampant foliage and deep shadows. The use of figures adds a sense of grandeur to the scene.

Robert Carlyle published in 1835, one year before Allom's painting, copies of drawings of six different views of Furness Abbey that are shown in Figures 8–13. These also provide us with a very personal and highly subjective interpretation of the ruin but, in contrast with Turner's and Allom's drawings, they were included in a more scholarly work, *Six Views of Furness Abbey with a condensed History and Description of the Monastery.*[25] The views can still be described as picturesque, but the architectural detail is given more emphasis. A bare outline of the history; the description of the ruins, taken directly from Thomas West's 1805 edition of *Antiquities of Furness*; and an accompanying ground plan of the abbey site, are all included on the first five pages. On each of the last six pages of this very slim volume is one pictorial view of the abbey ruins. The fact that these were given such prominence by the author is evident by the size of the book, eleven inches in width and fourteen and a half inches in height. The drawings are fairly accurate depictions of the buildings, but each one is a typical example of the Picturesque movement with all its attributes, still popular in the 1830s.

Carlyle, 'Furness Abbey from the School House'. [Figure 11]

Figure 8 locates Furness Abbey firmly in the landscape. It also includes peasant figures and cows in the foreground, probably to give it perspective and to underline the pastoral elements of the abbey grounds. The abbey buildings themselves rise gracefully out of the vegetation, as if part of

R. Carlyle, 'Furne
Abbey from the
South West'.
[Figure 12]

nature, and the surrounding trees produce a frame for the whole. In Figure 11 the people are still present, but this time they appear to represent visitors to the ruin, and the impression given is of a leisurely outing for a small group of friends who have come to the abbey for an enjoyable day trip. Drawing the eye into the centre of the picture is an abundance of foliage that adorns the walls. As we have seen, the early artists often added more greenery than was actually there in order to enhance the picturesque qualities.

The view of the five arches in the cloister, shown in Figure 12, above, includes two men who serve to endow the structure with a sense of grandeur as the buildings are seen to tower up behind the smaller figures. One of the men is pointing into the vestibule entrance to the chapter house doorway which, together with their dress, suggests that they are gentlemen with an interest in the ruin rather than working men using the ruin as grazing land or shelter for their animals.

Figure 9 has a similar group of early tourists in the foreground, one of whom is pointing to the ruins and turning to his friends. Again, illustrated by their dress, we can see that they are likely to have been of the 'gentry' class, especially when compared to the dress of the man, woman and two children shown in Figure 10. Figure 9 also shows the

. Carlyle, 'Furness Abbey from the Iorth'. [Figure 13]

natural line of the hillside which was disturbed by the later construction of the railway. In Figure 10 there are oddments of sculpture on the ground in the interior of the chapter house; these all add to the picturesque view, but also tell us that the site had not been cleared by the second quarter of the nineteenth century when these drawings were executed. The three cows in the final view of this collection, Figure 13, above, conveys to the observer the pastoral nature of the scene and the fact that the ruin is now viewed as the home of animals rather than of monks. All the figures included in the drawings are not mere shadows but are definitely intended to be part of the picture. Yet the above drawing also shows great accuracy in recording the extent of the damage caused by destruction and decay. Several pieces of masonry on the upper parts of the great north window, part of the crossing arch and the lantern tower are no longer there. In the 1920s the gap shown on the right hand side was rebuilt and the buttress and wall of the roofed outbuilding, both post-Dissolution features, have now disappeared. Carlyle's view of the north transept is a classic view of the abbey and typical of the period. This record is therefore of great value to the archaeologist as evidence of parts of the fabric that have disappeared or appeared since 1829.

In fact the level of detail in these drawings is impressive, and the importance Carlyle attaches to them in his short, and very visual, work is evident. His intention was probably to show the ruins at their decorative best, within the sphere of nature and indicative of his times, but also to leave a record of the detail of the architecture. Anyone who is familiar with Furness Abbey would be able to recognise the ruins from these drawings. Apart from the first image, the pictures are all focused closely on the buildings. The mixture of the scholarly and the artistic works well and can still be a source of pleasure to even the least romantic amongst us. However, it is not clear whether Gilpin, from a previous generation, would have approved of these drawings. He was of the opinion that any detailed representation of a ruin detracted from the 'natural' elements of the scene, and his own sketches were very much 'a glimpse of the ideal'.[26] He 'removed' anything which, in his opinion, muddied the composition. However, he agreed that the inclusion of cattle 'add[s] great variety, and animation to the scene'.[27]

The first-hand experience of the early tourist was often aided by the various 'travelling companions' which were published in the eighteenth and nineteenth centuries. Some of these will be analysed in more detail in Chapter Four with regard to their popularity and interpretation by the tourist. However, many of them incorporated romantic and picturesque drawings or engravings as illustrations of the places they described. In the last two decades of the eighteenth century, these drawings and engravings, which were an extension of the first 'tinted drawings' usually made to complement a topographical account of an area, tended to become more picturesque in their appearance. There was a risk that the process of print-making itself served to render some of the prints inaccurate, especially because the engraver, not the artist, was often the last person to check the proofs, and quality could vary greatly.[28]

The more academic works of the antiquarians also used drawings of buildings and other artefacts interwoven into their pages. These visual sources were not necessarily architectural line drawings, but were often enhanced by the use of the picturesque techniques that landscape artists such as Turner had developed. For example in 1844, the antiquarian Thomas Alcock Beck, who will be discussed further in Chapter Three, included picturesque drawings in his substantial scholarly work.[29] Beck's history has been consulted many times by academics since its publication and has not been impaired by the use of romantic images, examples of which can be seen in Figures 14 and 15.[30] The drawings were executed by Henry Shaw (1800–73) and engraved by John Le Keux, Senior (1783–1846). The guest hall chapel illustrated in Figure 14 has a soft, blurred outline that enhances the picturesque effect. Furthermore the foliage is obscuring much of the architectural detail even though this detail was an important element in Beck's scholarly appraisal.

The western tower in Figure 15 incorporates all the picturesque

Furness Abbey, ,uest hall, drawn by H. Shaw, ngraved by John Le Keux, Snr. [Figure 14]

techniques, including the use of animals, vegetation, stormy skies and even a shadowy figure of a shepherd. This is another of Shaw's drawings from the first half of the nineteenth century. Le Keux's engraving of the drawing was still used much later in a work written by W. H. St John Hope. Hope was an antiquarian scholar who, in the late nineteenth century and early twentieth century, excavated the site of Furness Abbey and wrote up his findings in learned journals.[31] Hope also included several romantic pictorial images of the architecture of Furness Abbey to illustrate an article he wrote which was published in the journal *The Builder* in 1895.[32] The artist, A. Beresford Pite, drew one of the images which is shown on page 27 (Figure 16). The drawing is very reminiscent of the 1840s and bears a remarkable resemblance to those of Carlyle, referred to above. The inclusion of several shadowy figures is typical of the picturesque image, but the architectural detail is fairly accurate and the buildings dominate the picture, indicating that the article was aimed at the professional.

In 1880 another scholarly history appeared in two volumes, written by Joseph Richardson, and entitled *Furness, Past and Present: Its History and Antiquities*. This book contains a picture of the chapter house doorway, Figure 17, which has been described as one of the most picturesque of

Furness Abbey, western tower, drawn by H. Shaw, engraved by John Le Keux, Snr. [Figure 15]

Top: A. Beresford Pite, Furness from the south-west angle of the cloister. [Figure 16]
Bottom: R. J. Hamerton, 'Norman Arch'. [Figure 17]

all the views of Furness Abbey.[33] The 'romantic' mood is created by the depiction of two gentlemen taking a respite from their walk around the abbey grounds. This is a hand-tinted etching, very finely executed, perfectly proportioned and showing the vegetation which still adorned the walls. It is, however, interesting to observe that iron railings enclose the entrance to three of the five Norman arches. This is an early indication of the use of the site by tourists. It is known that the owners of the site, the Cavendish family, were at this time concerned about vandalism, mainly from graffiti, and the gate into the chapter house would possibly have been locked at night.

Figure 18 is another plate taken from Richardson's second volume.[34] It is an attractive etching of the abbey and the neighbouring nineteenth-century hotel, executed by W. J. Welch. This was used at the head of a chapter of his book. If the intention had been to portray the hotel accurately, a photograph would have been more realistic, but the author chose, deliberately, to include a romantic view and to change the position of the hotel relative to the abbey to create a more picturesque image.

Many more examples of this style of interpretation could be cited, given that there are many picturesque drawings and paintings of Furness Abbey to be found in archives and libraries. Just one more image has been included, however, to illustrate the fact that the picturesque interpretation of the abbey was still very much in evidence as late as the 1930s. In a work, by J. Cuming Walters (1863–1933), published in 1930 and

W. J. Welch, Furness Abbey Hotel and the ruins. [Figure 18

ank Greenwood, Furness Abbey. [Figure 19]

entitled, very aptly, *The Charm of Lancashire*, there is a hand-tinted pencil drawing of the cloisters by Frank Greenwood, a Manchester artist (Figure 19, above).[35] The foliage is still visible, although by the 1930s the Office of Works were responsible for and maintained the site, and the stones would have been carefully cleared of any vegetation. The broken gate in the foreground mirrors the broken buildings, which adds to the aesthetic quality. In his work, Walters states that he 'only venture[s] to put impression before exactitude, and while [he] would not wittingly state a falsity, [he] prefer[s] a correct idea to a meticulously correct figure'.[36] He 'courteously' directs his readers to other works if they are searching for 'statistics, dimensions, lengths and breadths'. He argues that he has 'forsaken the well-worn and familiar highways for the more elusive and glamorous byways of romance'.[37] Walters was an editor, author and journalist, but he clearly identified himself with the cult of the picturesque from an earlier age when he says: '"charm" may be a harmony of picturesqueness, of historic association, of romantic interest; though each may suffice, the blend is irresistible'.[38]

Art produced the visual image of ruins but it was also through the language of poetry and prose that the romantic image of ruins was created. Romantic literature embraced both the depiction of the supernatural forces of nature embodied in the work of poets such as William Wordsworth (1770–1850), and the search for sensation to be found in the writers of Gothic novels. Language was used to encourage passive observers of landscapes to use their internal vision: their imagination. The scene drawn by the writer differed from the artist's representation in that it produced an awareness of movement and sound, of vibrant life and the changing colours and textures with which nature is richly endowed. The writer's view of the landscape was that it was more 'immediate, visual and sensuous' than that represented in the pictorial view.[39] These writers invested their work with highly personal emotions which they wished to share with others. They sensed the spirit of a place, and, as with the pictorial images of the era, the ruin in the landscape was an important element of this sentiment. In 1821 Wordsworth composed a sonnet which he called 'Old Abbeys', and two lines of this illustrate his romantic view of a ruined abbey and how it stimulated his imagination: 'Once ye were holy, ye are holy still;/ Your spirit freely let me drink and live.'[40]

The English Romantic Movement was greatly influenced by the publication in 1798 of *Lyrical Ballads*, a joint work written by William Wordsworth and Samuel Taylor Coleridge. This work influenced and nourished the romantic view of life which represented a movement away from the rational approach to the world to which previous generations had aspired. Wordsworth believed, as he stated himself in the preface to *Lyrical Ballads*, that poetry

> takes its origin from emotion recollected in tranquillity: the emotion is contemplated till, by a series of re-action, the tranquillity gradually disappears, and an emotion, kindred to that which was before the subject of contemplation, is gradually produced, and does itself actually exist in the mind.

These emotions were often of a sentimental nature. This is evident in Wordsworth's *The Prelude*, written between 1799 and 1805, an autobiographical account of his early life, which was, after half a century of reflections and alterations, published posthumously in 1850. According to Peter Quennell, Wordsworth's boyhood was 'the "seed-time" ... the time when, under the spell of lakes and mountains, he began to feel and think'.[41] Wordsworth believed that a child 'saw' the natural world through eyes that were unsullied by the later experiences which often prejudiced the adult's vision. Through the memories of his own childhood, with both its delightful and traumatic adventures, Wordsworth recaptured the insight of youth. Salvesen indicates that a strong theme running through Wordsworth's poetry is a 'connection of landscape with particular events and occasions'.[42] He goes on to argue that Wordsworth demonstrated this through his memories of his own past, and that there was a growing awareness of the past in society generally. This memory was often strongly infused with nostalgia.[43]

Wordsworth is closely associated with the Lake District, his home region, and much of his work is centred on this part of England. He was familiar with Furness Abbey and he composed two poems that incorporated the ruins as their central theme. In *The Prelude*, Wordsworth describes a boyhood excursion to the abbey on horseback, an adventure with 'mock-heroic overtones, involving a degree of unruliness'.[44] Wordsworth summons up the image of a ruin by using such terms as 'fractured' when referring to an arch or when he includes the word 'mouldering', purveying a sense of slow decay, especially when contrasted with the 'living trees': '... a mouldering pile with fractured arch,/Belfry, and images, and living trees;/A holy scene!'[45] His reference to a 'holy scene' tells us that Wordsworth admired the ruin with a certain amount of awe and reverence. He identifies with the image before him and instils in it an almost mystical sense of solitude when he uses words like 'sequestered', 'silent' and 'motionless' to describe the ruins and surrounding trees as they stand in the valley. These are the emotions he feels himself, and he contrasts them with the more violent forces of nature to be found in the 'tumultuous ocean' and the 'west wind' which he had left behind:

> Left by the west wind sweeping overhead
> From a tumultuous ocean, trees and towers
> In that sequestered valley may be seen,
> Both silent and both motionless alike;
> Such the deep shelter that is there, and such
> The safeguard for repose and quietness.[46]

Wordsworth and his friends soon shrug off the melancholy feelings, however, and, perhaps a little irreverently, he communicates excitement and movement when he takes us back to the adventure and the pace of the poetry picks up:

> Our steeds remounted and the summons given,
> With whip and spur we through the chauntry flew
> In uncouth race, and left the cross-legged knight,
> And the stone-abbot, ...[47]

Yet before the youths 'scampered homeward', there is time for more sober reflection, this time on the ruins as a place of decay – sad and vulnerable – as nature reclaims what was once a noble place:

> The earth was comfortless, and, touched by faint
> Internal breezes, sobbings of the place
> And respirations, from the roofless walls
> The shuddering ivy dripped large drops – yet still
> So sweetly 'mid the gloom the invisible bird
> Sang to herself, that there I could have made
> My dwelling place, and lived for ever there
> To hear such music.[48]

Wordsworth ends his interpretation of the ruins on a more positive note when he talks of the wren. He conveys the suffering of the ruins by his reference to 'sobbings', but then tells us of how his spirits were lifted by the confidence of youth, when he heard the 'singing' of the bird. Nature does not, it seems, lament for long.

The sense of destruction that the ruins convey to Wordsworth is re-examined in another poem written some years later, in 1814. Here Wordsworth is alluding to the foundation charter of Furness Abbey when he says:

> The stars of human glory are cast down;
> Perish the roses and the flowers of kings,
> Princes, and emperors, and the crowns and palms
> Of all the mighty, withered and consumed![49]

Compare these lines with a translation of part of the foundation charter which Stephen, Count of Boulogne and Mortain granted to the monks at Furness in 1127. This states, rather prophetically, before the granting of the land is recorded:

> Considering every day the uncertainty of life, that roses and flowers of kings, emperors and dukes, and the crowns and palms of all the great wither and decay: and that all things, with an uninterrupted course, tend to dissolution and death.[50]

Wordsworth returned to Furness Abbey in the summer of 1845 to witness the construction of the railway that was to bring the tourists to his hallowed spot. In a short poem he describes how the railway labourers, taking their lunch break, may have viewed the abbey. The interpretation is Wordsworth's, but his language is so vivid that we can imagine the wonder which the ruins evoked when the navvies contemplated the architecture. They too, it seems, felt the spirit of the ruins and the reference to the 'Profane Despoilers' is Wordsworth's reproof for those responsible for the building of the railway which he, and many of his contemporaries, lamented.

> Others look up, and with fixed eyes admire
> That wide-spanned arch, wondering how it was raised,

To keep, so high in air, its strength and grace:
All seem to feel the spirit of the place,
And by the general reverence God is praised:
Profane Despoilers, stand ye not reproved,
While thus these simple-hearted men are moved?[51]

Another manifestation of the ruin in the literature of the late eighteenth and early nineteenth centuries was an interest in Gothic architecture and the Gothic novel. The Gothic novel was part of the Romantic movement, and reference to Furness Abbey and the works of Ann Radcliffe (1764–1823) will illustrate the role of the ruin in this genre. Mrs Radcliffe, as she was popularly known, enjoyed European success at the end of the eighteenth century with such novels as *A Sicilian Romance*. Gothic architecture, and in particular that of castles and abbeys, was an important feature of Mrs Radcliffe's novels. For example, in *A Sicilian Romance*, Mrs Radcliffe sets part of the narrative in the abbey of St Augustin, which she says:

> was a large magnificent mass of Gothic architecture, whose gloomy battlements, and majestic towers arose in proud sublimity from amid the darkness of the surrounding shades. It was founded in the twelfth century, and stood a proud monument of monkish superstition and princely magnificence.[52]

She appears to make the abbey 'male' and unfriendly, a departure from the usual notion of abbeys as places of safety and refuge. Mrs Radcliffe, however, wrote in an age when the traveller was in search of excitement, even danger. It was the thrill of the sublime that she exploited.

Mrs Radcliffe herself was a keen traveller and a lover of picturesque scenery. She envisaged landscapes as '"archetypes" of human emotions',[53] and her travel journal (which was subsequently published), of a trip she made through Europe in 1794, included a tour of the Lake District during which she visited Furness Abbey. It is worth quoting some of her description of the ruins here:

> The deep retirement of its situation, the venerable grandeur of its gothic arches, and the luxuriant, yet ancient trees that shadow this forsaken spot, are circumstances of picturesque, and if the expression may be allowed, of sentimental beauty, which fill the mind with solemn, yet delightful emotion ... Its romantic gloom, and sequestered privacy, particularly adapted it to the austerities of monastic life.[54]

Evidently Mrs Radcliffe saw the ruin as a picturesque image, a vision which evoked certain emotions. However her reference to the monks shows that she also appreciated what the ruins had once represented. Her interpretation of the abbey was every bit as graphic and meaningful as the artist's or the poet's imagery. She described what she saw, whilst subtly embellishing it. The ruin, to Mrs Radcliffe, was endowed with a 'sense of place' or a 'sense of spirituality', appropriate because it was built to the glory of God, but as a ruin it now possessed its own ethereal quality which had nothing to do with its original purpose.

Mrs Radcliffe's description of the area has similarities with those contained in many of the guides that were printed in the nineteenth century to aid the traveller through unfamiliar country. They were highly descriptive and encompassed the poetic and rather flowery language of this era. Although some of these guides and short histories will be examined in more detail in Chapter Four, one, which was published by Francis Evans in 1842, can be used as an example of the picturesque and romantic point of view.[55] A tour of Furness Abbey is included and this commences with a very 'picturesque' description of the ruins. Evans says:

> 'A Temple, in possession of regular symmetry', observes an elegant writer, 'is beautiful; when broken into parts, it is picturesque; when falling into ruins, it is sublime. For, as patience is the greatest of friends to the unfortunate, so is time the greatest of friends to the lover of landscape. It resolves the noblest works of art into the most affecting ornaments of created things.'[56]

Evans then described the sensation of looking at the ruins as

> being inspired with a hallowed sensibility, which, whilst it causes the heart to melt as if awakened from the contemplation of a melancholy, yet delightful, dream, adds purity and taste to the emotions of grandeur and sublimity in the soul.[57]

Yet Evans argued that it is not just the images provoked by the ruins of the abbey which could create strong emotions; he also believed that the monks felt similar emotions when they viewed the building at a time when it was whole and in use. After a description of the inside of the Church and the 'theatrical pomp' with which he believed the services were conducted, he speculates on how the monk's devotion was:

> calculated to awaken in the mind [and] could not fail to produce the most intense emotions of sublimity, grandeur, reverence and awe, softened indeed, but not diminished, by the solemn harmonies of the 'full-voic'd' choir.[58]

Another example in the same year can be seen in a monthly magazine entitled *An Illustrated Itinerary of the County of Lancaster*. The compilers of this periodical were attempting to fill a gap in the publication of itineraries by 'combining descriptions of scenery and antiquities with living manners and characteristics'.[59] One of these magazines included a description of Furness Abbey's ruins which was part scholarly but was much more representative of the romantic style. The ruins were portrayed as being surrounded by trees which:

> add much to the impressive aspect by causing numerous changes of light and shade, often overshadowing windows through which the eye takes in dark arches and intervening lights with bits of exquisite beauty for pictorial effect.[60]

This is an example of a pictorial interpretation of the ruins by the use of language imbued with a great deal of sentiment. The same sentimental view of the ruins is also very evident in a short booklet entitled *A Trip to Furness Abbey and Windermere* written by a self-professed 'sentimentalist' in 1845.[61] The writer starts the account of his travels by stating that: 'We are true lovers of nature – enthusiastic worshippers at her shrine, whether the image be a beautiful woman or a butterfly.' The image we are concerned with here is that of the ruins of Furness Abbey, a visit to which was on the writer's itinerary. However, he states that it is important to visit the ruins in the evening because:

> the calm summer's evening, the pale moonlight, the sound of the distant waves faintly breaking upon the shore, and the melancholy cry of the corn-crake, all conspired to prepare our mind with a feeling of solemn delight, for the enjoyment of our visit to those time-honoured walls of which we have heard so much.[62]

The writer describes his own, and his friends' reaction to the ruins. He talks of the sadness the ruins evoked, and the atmosphere the moonbeams created by throwing light and shade on to the broken remains. This had the effect of banishing the signs of decay which, he says, 'the glare of the sunshine renders so prominent'.[63] They then embark on a fantasy trip where their imagination conjures up the ghosts of a party of knights and a baron who were visiting the abbey. Together with their ladies the ghosts enter the church where they are met by the abbot, and 'rich offerings are made, and the shrine is lit up, and amidst the pealing of the anthem, the waving of censers, and toll of the bell, that goodly train disappears from the church'.[64] This romantic vision is further enhanced by an account of a beautiful maiden. The vision is, once again, a product of the travellers' imaginations as they sit on the carved seats of the sedilia bathed in moonlight. She enters the church and, kneeling before the abbot's chair, she 'raises her large blue eyes, berimmed with tears. Her cherry lip trembles and her bosom heaves with solemn emotion.'[65]

The genuine pleasure these travellers derive from the ruins is very apparent in the writing. This visit to the Lake District, we are told at the beginning of the account, was taken by men who worked in a little office in a dark back-street 'with its one window and high stool, without cushion', and who felt that, by using part of their wages to fund their holiday, they would find 'sunshine and quiet and a twelvemonths' stock of health'.[66] The journey was made on horseback in the middle of August, and, although published in 1845, the account may have been written, perhaps in a travel diary, some years before.

This romantic image is also reflected in the poetry of the time and, in a book entitled *Bygone Lancashire*, edited by Ernest Axon and published in 1892, great emphasis is placed on the poets' vision of Furness Abbey. The poems of two nineteenth-century poets, Aubrey Thomas de Vere (1814–1902) and Samuel Longfellow (1819–92) are included in this publication. Both poets had visited the abbey and were moved to interpret what they saw in the language of poetry.

De Vere was a poet, essayist and critic. He was a friend of Wordsworth, and his poetry contains the same simple language as the Lakeland poet who had obviously influenced his own writing. In his poem on Furness Abbey, de Vere laments the loss of the monastery and underscores its religious aspect. He begins his sonnet with the following lines:

> God with a mighty and outstretched hand,
> Stays thee from sinking and ordains to be
> His witness lifted 'twixt the Irish sea
> And that still beauteous, once faith-hallowed land
> Stand as a sign, monastic prophet stand![67]

De Vere seemed to see the existence of the ruins as a moral warning of the power of God, who allowed the ruins to remain almost as a reproach for man's failings – not least for man's part in its original destruction.

Samuel Longfellow's vision of Furness Abbey portrayed the romance of past history: another facet of the rejection of the rational and scientific view of the world. Longfellow, like Wordsworth before him, was inspired by a portion of the abbey's foundation charter. His poem emphasises the past use of the ruins as a working monastery, but mourns its demise, which he sees as evidence of the fragility of man when compared to the more enduring power of God. He says:

> So fade the roses and the flowers of kings,
> And crown and palms decay with humbler things;
> All works built up by toil of mortal breath
> Tend in unbroken course to dust and death.

However, whilst Longfellow interprets the ruin as a reproach for the past deeds of men, which a latter-day preacher might use as an example of man's folly, he also sees the ruins as picturesque – a view fit for painters and poets:

> Yet spare for tender thought, for beauty spare,
> Some sculptured capital, some carving fair,

Yon ivied archway, fit for poet's dream,
For painter's pencil, or for preacher's theme![68]

A final example of the poets' interpretation is provided by an anonymous writer who, in 1895, penned a romantic poem entitled *A Pleasure Trip to Furness Abbey by the Steamer, 'The Duchess of Lancaster'*, part of which was set at Furness Abbey.[69] The tale told was of a pleasure trip to the abbey on 13 July 1848. The author was one of the participants, all of whom embarked from Lancaster on two steamers, the 'Duchess of Lancaster' and the 'John Denistown', on a journey of adventure which is recounted in the form of a poem. We take up the story as the party arrived at the abbey on the newly completed railway track. The writer is concerned when he compares the decay of the ruins with the newness of the railway station, which seemed to him, as it had to Wordsworth three years before, as being out of keeping with his view of the ruins. He describes the railway, which had brought his friends to the site, as 'displeasing'. He observes that:

The Abbey on the one hand see
  All the mouldering to decay;
And on the other, glittering bright,
  A railway station, gay.

The poem goes on to describe the blossoming of a romance between two of the trippers, Henry and Emilie. Emilie, we are informed, had fallen down the steps leading up to the western tower. The account continues:

Now Henry next with gentlest care
  Took off the lady's glove; [which was torn when she fell]
And wish'd, of course, that hand were his,
  And fell headlong in love.

This charming story makes little reference to the history of the site and provides little description of the ruins, but a theme emerges of a very delightful day out for a group of tourists which was so memorable that the writer was moved to write it down, in a manner reminiscent of Wordsworth, in a poem nearly fifty years later. The site of an abbey, it appears, had once again cast its magical spell and had become the scene of a romantic interlude.

However, during the nineteenth century when this poem was written, as Norman Nicholson argues, the 'Picturesque was already becoming a planned pleasure, a Butlin camp of the sensibilities, with all its possibilities tasted, tested, tried, recorded and mapped out.'[70] The picturesque of the eighteenth century was a matter of aesthetics which developed into one of sensation, and later into one of romanticism. However, by the middle of the nineteenth century the Picturesque was giving way to the more scientific view favoured by John Ruskin. The imagination, that could so distort the actual image, was now becoming unfashionable, and the Victorian tourist wanted more factual information. This was provided by maps, engravings, postcards and guidebooks. The arrival of the railway provided the accessibility that past generations had not enjoyed; the Lakes were no longer isolated and therefore seemed less wild and unpredictable. Writers like Harriet Martineau (1802–76) 'realised that to condemn the people of the Lakes to an unnatural, archaic existence in an artificial, preserved countryside was both economically absurd and morally wrong'.[71]

Through literature we have seen how this sense of the past – the view that the abbey is a monument that is part of our history – was developing. Ruins were beginning to represent a past that needed investigating, and this could be seen in the antiquarian pursuits of the period. The time was ripe for the Lake District to become the domain of the geologist, the botanist and, in particular, the archaeologist and the antiquarian. This development will be explored in more detail in the next chapter.

Notes

1. Quote from G. Simmel in Roth, Lyons and Merewether, *Irresistible Decay*, p. 44.
2. R. W. Harris, *Romanticism and the Social Order, 1780–1830* (London, 1969), p. 11.
3. J. R. Watson, *Picturesque Landscape and English Romantic Poetry* (London, 1970), p. 12.
4. Quote from J. Addison, in M. Andrews, *The Search for the Picturesque: Landscape Aesthetics and Tourism in Britain, 1760–1800* (Aldershot, 1990), p. vii.
5. Watson, *Picturesque Landscape*, p. 12.
6. Andrews, *Search for the Picturesque*, p. 41.
7. Nicholson, *Lakers*, p. 44.
8. Ibid., p. 40.
9. Gilpin, *Observations on the Mountains and Lakes*, p. 188.
10. Roth, Lyons and Merewether, *Irresistible Decay*, p. 3.
11. Andrews, *Search for the Picturesque*, p. 46.
12. M. W. Thompson, *Ruins: Their Preservation and Display* (London, 1981), p. 15.
13. Nicholson, *Lakers*, p. 46.
14. R. Macaulay, *Pleasure of Ruins* (London, 1964), pp. 169–70.
15. Ibid., p. 26.
16. Simmel, in Roth, Lyons and Merewether, *Irresistible Decay*, p. 44.
17. Andrews, *Search for the Picturesque*, p. 102.
18. Gilpin, *Observations on the Mountains and Lakes*, p. 158.
19. Ibid., p. 156: drawing of Furness Abbey by Mr John Smith. Gilpin says of this artist that '[he] has had a principal hand in etching the drawings which accompany these observations' (p. 157).
20. J. M. W. Turner, *Furness Abbey*, Tate Gallery, London.

21. *Handbook to the Abbey of St Mary of Furness in Lancashire* (Ulverston, 1845), between pp. 24–5.
22. J. M. W. Turner, *Tintern Abbey*, Ashmolean Museum, Oxford.
23. D. Hill, *Turner in the North: A Tour through Derbyshire, Yorkshire, Durham, Northumberland, The Scottish Borders, The Lake District, Lancashire and Lincolnshire in the year 1797* (Newhaven, 1996), pp. 56, 159.
24. F. Graham, *Picturesque Lancashire* (Newcastle-upon-Tyne, 1969), p. 63, plate 104.
25. R. Carlyle, *Six Views of the Ruins of Furness Abbey with a condensed History and Description of the Monastery* (London, 1835).
26. E. Moir, *The Discovery of Britain: The English Tourists, 1540–1840* (London, 1964), p. 124.
27. Ibid., p. 127.
28. The making of prints in the 18th and 19th centuries is a complex process. For a readable overview, see R. Russell, *Discovering Antique Prints* (Aylesbury, 1986). There is also a useful bibliography in this work, and a list of the leading engravers who were working in these two centuries.
29. Beck, *Annales Furnesienses.*
30. Ibid., opposite pp. 396, 374.
31. W. H. St John Hope, *The Abbey of St Mary in Furness* (Kendal, 1902), opposite p. 251.
32. W. H. St John Hope, 'Furness Abbey', *The Builder*, 6 Jul. 1895, pp. 10–13.
33. J. Richardson, *Furness, Past and Present: Its History and Antiquities* (Barrow-in-Furness, 1880), ii, opposite p. 132.
34. Ibid., ii, p. 117.
35. J. Cuming Walters, *The Charm of Lancashire* (2nd edn, London, 1930), opposite p. 62.
36. Ibid., p. xii.
37. Ibid., p. xi.
38. Ibid., p. 6.
39. C. Salvesen, *The Landscape of Memory: A Study of Wordsworth's Poetry* (London, 1965), p. 69.
40. W. Wordsworth, *Ecclesiastical Sonnets*, XXXV: 'Old Abbeys', ll. 13–14, in *The Works of William Wordsworth*, intro. A. Till (Ware, 1994), p. 449.
41. P. Quennell, *Romantic England: Writing and Painting, 1717–1851* (London, 1970), p. 63.
42. Salvesen, *Landscape of Memory*, p. 158.
43. Ibid., p. 173.
44. K. Hanley, 'Wordsworth's "Region of the Peaceful Self"', in K. Hanley and A. Milbank (eds), *From Lancaster to the Lakes: The Region in Literature* (Lancaster, 1992), p. 8.
45. W. Wordsworth, *The Prelude*, Book II: 'School-Time (continued)', ll. 105–7, in *Works*, p. 643.
46. Ibid., ll. 109–14.
47. Ibid., ll. 115–18, pp. 643–4.
48. Ibid., ll. 121–8, p. 644.
49. W. Wordsworth, *The Excursion*, Book VII: 'The Churchyard among the Mountains (continued)', ll. 979–82, in *Works*, p. 872.

50. J. P. Morris, *A Handy Guide to the Ruins of Furness Abbey*, rev. by J. Turner (Ulverston, *c.* 1855), p. 15.
51. W. Wordsworth, *Miscellaneous Sonnets*, XLVIII: 'At Furness Abbey', ll. 8–14, in *Works*, p. 283.
52. R. Miles, *Ann Radcliffe: The Great Enchantress* (Manchester, 1995), p. 94.
53. Ibid., p. 24.
54. J. Britton, *The Beauties of England and Wales; or Original Delineations, Topographical, Historical, and Descriptive, of each county* (London, 1807), ix, p. 85.
55. Evans, *Furness and Furness Abbey.*
56. Ibid., p. 197.
57. Ibid.
58. Ibid., p. 202.
59. *An Illustrated Itinerary of the County of Lancaster* (London, 1842), p. 325.
60. Ibid., p. 327.
61. H. H. David, *A Trip to Furness Abbey and Windermere by a Sentimentalist* (Kirkby Lonsdale, 1845).
62. Ibid., p. 29.
63. Ibid., p. 31.
64. Ibid., p. 32.
65. Ibid., p. 33.
66. Ibid., p. 3.
67. Quoted from A. T. de Vere, in E. Axon (ed.), *Bygone Lancashire* (London, 1892), p. 205.
68. Quoted from S. Longfellow, in Axon, *Bygone Lancashire*, p. 207.
69. *'A Pleasure Trip to Furness Abbey by the Steamer, 'The Duchess of Lancaster'*, 13 July 1848 (Lancaster, 1895).
70. Nicholson, *Lakers*, p. 63.
71. Ibid., p. 201.

CHAPTER THREE

The Scholarly Challenge: Antiquarians, Archaeologists and Historians

> Antiquity was exemplary, beneficial and beautiful. Yet its physical remains were in the main neglected or destroyed … Only in the nineteenth century did preservation evolve from an antiquarian, quirky, episodic pursuit into a set of national programmes, only in the twentieth has every country sought to secure its own heritage against despoliation and decay.
>
> [David Lowenthal] [1]

The cult of the past was at first primarily the concern of a small number of intellectuals but gradually, as the twentieth century progressed and understanding of the importance of history grew, this interest spread. Artefacts, including ruins, were now viewed as evidence that needed to be uncovered, preserved and reconstructed in an attempt to learn more. This chapter will assess the scholarly approach to Furness Abbey and how this has changed with increased knowledge and technical advances.

Charles Merewether argues that once ruins are 'uncovered they are irrevocably changed: they become part of the present'.[2] Awareness of ruins as a historical document brings them into the present, but their assessment and interpretation are subject to the values of the time in which they are being examined. However much we uncover, although our knowledge is increased, we will never fully understand the past because, as L. P. Hartley maintains, 'the past is a foreign country: they do things differently there'.[3] However, the fascination for trying to expose fragments of the past and, by so doing, to expose the 'truth', was becoming endemic by the nineteenth century.

A scholarly interest in ruins can be detected as early as the seventeenth century when Sir William Dugdale's *Monasticon Anglicanum* was published in three volumes between 1655 and 1673. Although the information collected by Dugdale was taken from the extant documentary evidence, and monastic architecture was largely ignored, it provided a base from which monastic studies could grow. The first interest in the buildings themselves was stimulated by the emergence of the Picturesque movement, as outlined in Chapter Two. At this time the need to preserve the remains also became an issue.

Topographical interest can be seen in the work of two early topographers, Samuel and Nathaniel Buck, who produced engravings of many of the ruins of England and Wales. These plates were included in the brothers' *Antiquities: or Venerable Remains of above Four Hundred Castles, Monasteries, Palaces etc. in England and Wales* which was published between 1726 and 1742 in seventeen annual parts.

An awareness of, and interest in, the past was also disseminated through the publication of county histories and topographical books; this interest also led to the proliferation of national and regional antiquarian societies throughout the nineteenth century. The Victoria County Histories, launched in 1899, provided, often in several volumes, an overview of the historical, geographical, geological and botanical details of a particular county, and included an archaeological survey of known historical sites.[4] Four antiquarian and archaeological societies of particular importance in the north of England were the Chetham Society which formed in 1843, the Historic Society of Lancashire and Cheshire founded in 1848, the Cumberland and Westmorland Antiquarian and Archaeological Society founded in 1866, and the Lancashire and Cheshire Antiquarian Society founded in 1883. All published widely, their writings being researched, written and edited by antiquarians, usually churchmen and gentlemen with scholarly interests. They were willing to spend time, often their leisure time, in seeking out and collecting artefacts and documents which helped them to learn about the past. For example, using such gentlemen scholars to do much of his research, Edward Baines (1774–1848) published a history of Lancashire in four volumes in 1836. Philippa Levine states that the nature of these men (they were invariably men) was to share their knowledge with others of a like mind. She says: 'Many of the county societies saw their major function as being the collective organisations in which successful local history could come to fruition.'[5]

The early historians, including the architectural historians with their interest in buildings rather than what went on inside them, formed a distinct group which was developing its own character throughout the nineteenth century. The historian was usually university educated and often worked in academia although, because history as a discipline was still not fully established, they were not inevitably scholars in the history departments of the institutions in which they worked. Although they were not necessarily more scholarly in their approach to research, they tended to perceive themselves as 'more professional' and had a 'need to dissociate themselves from the amateur world of antiquarian interests'.[6]

A much smaller group in the nineteenth century were the archaeologists. By the second decade of the nineteenth century, the tentative excavation of monastic sites had begun.[7] Closely tied to the antiquarian's pursuits,

ght: Photograph of the east prospect of the ruins, 1998. [Figure 20]

low: S. and N. Buck, Furness Abbey, 1727. [Figure 21]

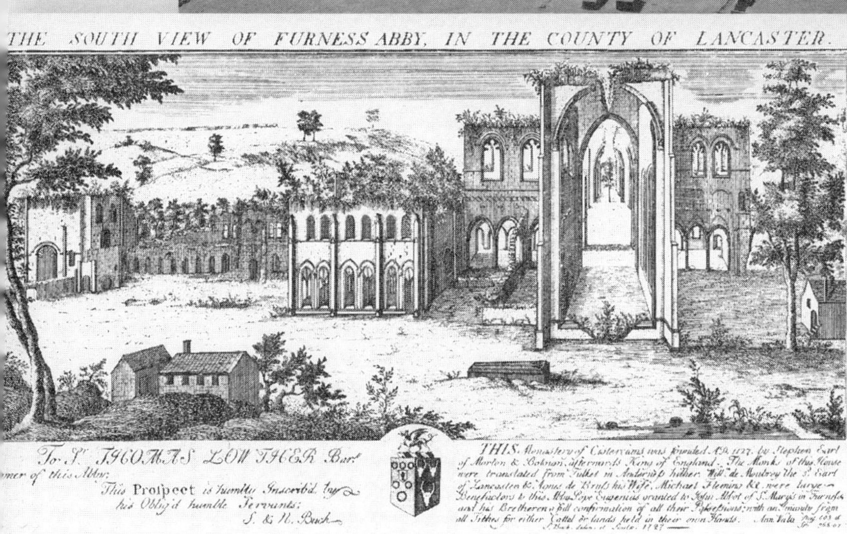

it was a constant struggle for them to establish themselves as a separate group with their own objectives. However, as the century progressed, they tended to focus specifically on artefacts and material remains and were especially involved in excavation, particularly of ruins. Initially their science and methods were very inexact, and the thrill of digging up the past tended to be seen by some as an exciting pastime which, as Levine argues, caused 'damage and desecration arising from careless excavation and primitive techniques'.[8]

By the end of the nineteenth century, the overlap between the activities of the 'antiquarian', the 'historian', and the 'archaeologist' was becoming

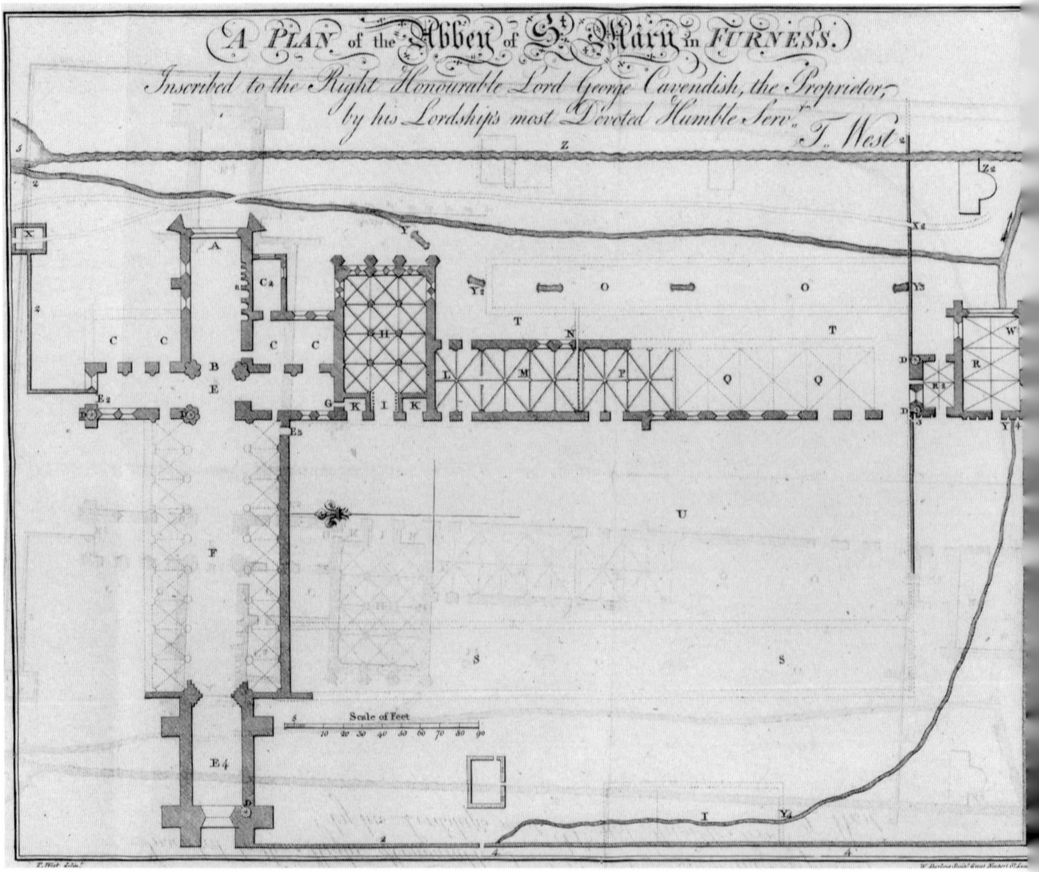

T. West, plan o
Furness Abbey,
1774. [Figure 22

less blurred. Levine says that by the 1880s the 'antiquarians' were acquiring the status of amateurs and the 'archaeologist' and 'historian' were emerging as 'trained and respected professional[s]'.[9]

When the Lancashire Victoria County History was published in eight volumes between 1906 and 1914, several historians contributed to it by using their professional skills. James Tait and F. M. Powicke were two of these professional men.[10]

Architects too were beginning to express an interest in medieval monastic remains, illustrated by the 'Gothic Revival' in building during the nineteenth century and by 1859, the Cistercians were being heralded as 'missionaries of Gothic'.[11] The definition of Gothic architecture is complex and not all monastic remains can be termed Gothic. A variety of terms for differing methods of ecclesiastical construction were used in many of the older publications and this has served to confuse the issue further, although Thomas Rickman (1776–1841) in his book *Attempt to Discriminate the Styles of English Architecture*, published in 1819, made a reasonably successful attempt to formulate a standard means of naming individual architectural styles.

All these diverse groups of intellectuals – the antiquarians, the historians, the archaeologists and the architects – had an interest in abbey ruins, and it is their interpretation of these ruins, and of Furness Abbey in particular, which will now be examined.

The progress of the intellectual interpretation of ruins can be traced through an analysis of the texts produced since the Dissolution. In the present study, special emphasis will be placed on extant visual evidence in the form of drawings, paintings, photographs, cartographic evidence and ground plans. These images provide a valuable source of visual evidence as to how the ruins were explored and interpreted by scholars, and we will see how our comprehension of the past has been advanced by the development of various technologies, particularly during the twentieth century.

A very early scholarly interpretation of Furness Abbey can be found in the Buck brothers' work cited above. Their drawing of Furness Abbey is shown in Figure 21, and is dated 1727.[12] It is labelled as a south view of Furness Abbey, which is misleading. It is in fact an engraving of the east prospect of the ruins. A recent photograph of the same view is shown above it. The Buck drawings have been cited in many learned works since they were produced in 1727, exactly six hundred years after the founding of the abbey. The drawings constitute an important document for the historian because the Buck brothers were endeavouring to record the detail of the architecture rather than reproducing a picturesque interpretation. It can therefore serve as a record of those parts of the abbey that no longer exist. For example, a comparison with the modern photograph (Figure 20) reveals that a large part of the head of the great east window has disappeared since the early part of the eighteenth century. The appearance of a wall on the left hand side, shown in the Buck drawing, was probably a post-Dissolution wall and was removed in the 1930s. No distinction is made, however, between the medieval building and post-Dissolution additions. Caution must also be exercised in interpreting such drawings as they are presented as flattened images and lack perspective.

Another early stimulus to the scholarly interest and understanding of monastic ruins was the drawing of plans that recorded the layout of the visible buildings. Those responsible for early sketch plans showed little interest in recording the whole site. Only the fragments that were seen above ground were documented and the existence of other buildings was merely speculated upon. Few questions were asked, and mistakes were made. For example it was assumed that all walls met at right angles and that all walls were of a similar thickness. More accurate evidence was only acquired, and specific architectural questions answered, as a result of the development of excavation.[13] Coppack argues that it was the recording and publication of these findings that was to contribute significantly to an understanding of monasticism and provide a permanent record of a particular site.[14]

The plans for Furness Abbey from 1774 onwards will now be analysed with a view to explaining and illustrating how their compilers have interpreted the remains and how an increase in knowledge has led to amendments to the plans over time. This knowledge was gained through observations, excavations, and through evidence obtained from other Cistercian monastic ruins that conformed to a similar plan to that of Furness. Norman Nicholson said of Furness Abbey that it was a

> text-book abbey, a large-scale model for the student, almost complete in the details of its foundation plan – church, chapter-house, cloisters, dormitories, infirmary, kitchen, abbot's lodging and even the drainage and sewage system.[15]

The motives for the inclusion of a plan in a particular publication varied. A plan could be used as an archaeological record with as much accuracy as possible or as a guide for the lay visitor who would want a plan that was easy to understand and follow. The plans that are included in this book have been chosen because they reflect the general trend in the development of antiquarian and archaeological pursuits over time, and because they represent some of the most important academic works of the period. A brief assessment of each of the works is therefore included, together with analysis of other visual evidence contained in the various publications.

As a tool to facilitate our understanding of how the plans included in this book have changed over the last two centuries, an abstract of six ground plans, chronologically displayed, appears in Plate 3. The first plan was drawn in 1774 by Thomas West (1720–79), a Jesuit and a topographer, and the sixth plan was published in 1998, by English Heritage, as a

W. Close, north-west view the abbey, *c.*18c [Figure 23]

component of their latest tourist guide to the abbey. For convenience, the plans have been simplified but all the plans referred to can be examined in more detail, as they are all included in this work. The changes result from subsequent excavations, more accurate measuring, and the acquisition of new knowledge.

The first publication to be considered is West's *The Antiquities of Furness*, first published in 1774. West's work is mostly devoted to a history of the abbey and includes the topography, economy and social conditions of the area, as well as a brief description of the abbey ruins. This work contains an engraving of the same view as that in the Buck brothers' drawing which is shown in Figure 21. West's engraving, produced as a foldout page, can be found facing page 1 in the first edition of that year and is labelled, more accurately, as 'The East Prospect of the Ruins of Furness Abbey in Lancashire'.[16]

West states in his preface that the early drawing by the Buck brothers should be complemented by the addition of a ground plan which, he continues, was the 'only thing wanting to give a just and satisfactory account of the whole, and to preserve its memory to future ages'. He then goes on to tell us that 'Nothing of this kind has been attempted before this, and those who visit the ruins return with a confused idea of the premises.'[17] West's intention was, therefore, to correct any past errors or misconceptions for anyone sufficiently interested in understanding what the ruins represented in terms of architectural analysis. In his preface, West expands even further on his motives for writing his book, including his intention to 'give pleasure to the curious, and satisfaction to those who visit the pompous ruins of Furness Abbey'.[18]

Figure 22 shows Thomas West's original plan of 1774, which is also included as the first representation in Plate 3.[19] His plan is quite accurately drawn and measured, but he was impeded by the fact that relatively little masonry survived above ground, and even that was covered by two centuries of undergrowth. Much of the rubble of centuries of disintegration lay in vast mounds throughout the site obscuring a great deal of what still remained.

West concentrated on the main buildings where substantial remains were visible and he did not attempt to excavate or clear the site. His observations were purely on what he could see. His plan included a sketchy explanation of the various parts of the site, identified by letters. For example his letter 'G' is 'a door from the dormitory by which the monks at midnight came into the church to sing Mattins or morning prayers': in other words, the night stairs, the very same ones that Turner sat on to execute his sketch (see Chapter Two, Figure 3). West speculates on the existence of further buildings, notably what are now known as the lay brothers quarters. West outlined, in grey, his estimate of the location of some of the missing foundations. However, when his plan is compared to subsequent plans, it can be seen that he has clearly overestimated the lengths of some buildings. West's walls tended to join up with other non-existent walls and the cloister is, as a consequence, far too large. The infirmary chapel, indicated by the letter 'R' and called the 'school house', has been drawn as if parallel to the rest of the claustral complex. As will be seen by a comparison with the plan of 1844, this is incorrect.

West was evidently grateful to the Cavendish family for allowing him to wander amid the ruins. He inscribed his substantial book, *The Antiquities of Furness*, to the Right Honourable Lord George Cavendish, who owned the site at this time. In his dedication West says, referring to Lord Cavendish, that since 'the study of antiquities is one of Your favourite walks, the choice of a patron is evidently justified'. In the opening dedication in the 1774 edition (and included in the subsequent editions) the motive for writing the history, namely that of preserving Furness Abbey as an important historical document, is clearly communicated to the reader. West says in his address to Lord Cavendish:

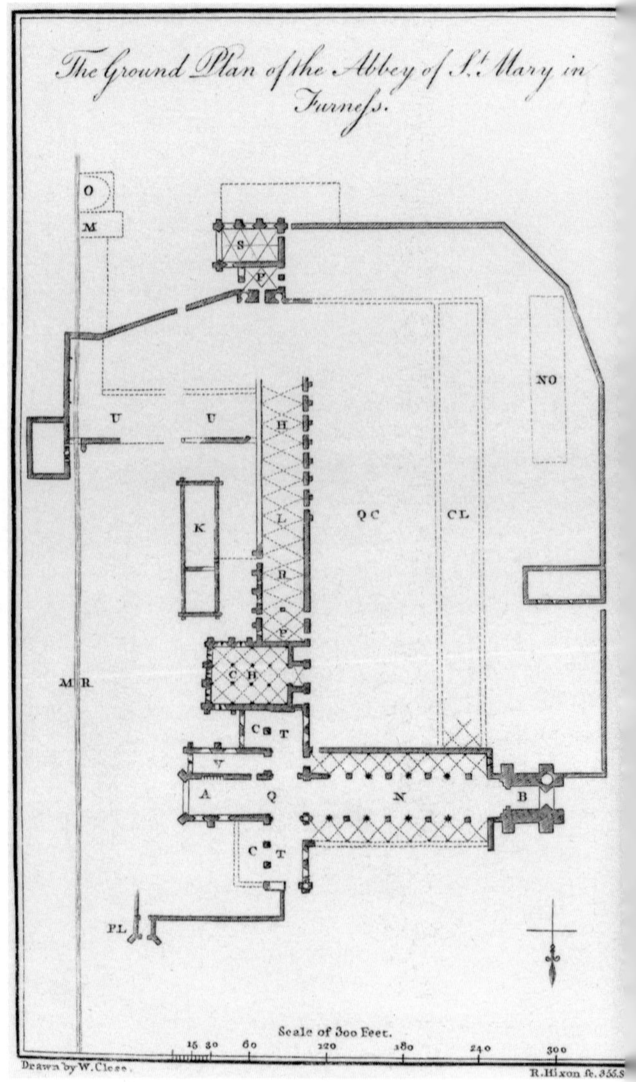

T. West, plan of Furness Abbey 1805 redrawn by W. Close. [Figure

> While to raise sinking industry is your chief care, your Abbey of Furness, once the pride of princes, and desire of Kings, long buried in ruins increased by mouldering, all devouring time, is now to be preserved by Your protection, a lasting monument of ancient grandeur, and religious pomp.[20]

This early reference to preservation does not necessarily indicate that Lord Cavendish intended to carry out any remedial work in order to preserve the ruins. It merely indicates an awareness that what was left of the monastery was important and needed to be recorded. West complains that Sir William Dugdale's work, *Monasticon Anglicanum*, is silent on

Furness Abbey, even though, West points out, more of the buildings were intact at that time. He expressed concern that the surviving buildings might be destroyed completely by the onset of time.[21]

The continuing value of West's work is shown by its revision as late as 1805 by William Close of Dalton (1776–1841). Close redrew West's plan and in 1805 published a new and edited version of West's work. Close was a surgeon by trade, but had an interest in topography and history. The new edition was supplemented by eighty-six additional pages which included two views of Furness Abbey drawn by Close himself, together with several new observations produced from his own research. This work was reprinted in 1813. His rather stark drawing of the north-west view of the abbey is shown in Figure 23. Although the drawing lacks detail, it is a fair architectural representation.[22] Close relates how, in 1796, the late Right Honourable Lord Frederick Cavendish, who, at that time, was the owner of the abbey, placed a strong buttress against the wall on the west side of the window in the north transept. This is an early tangible indication of the need to preserve the ruins.[23] The 1805 plan is a simplified version of West's 1774 plan. The site, Close states, has been remeasured. However, when both plans and their accompanying explanations are

Above: [R]econstruction of [th]e chapter house doorway, 1844. [Figure 25]

Right: Furness Abbey, chapter house doorway, [p]hotograph, 1998. [Figure 26]

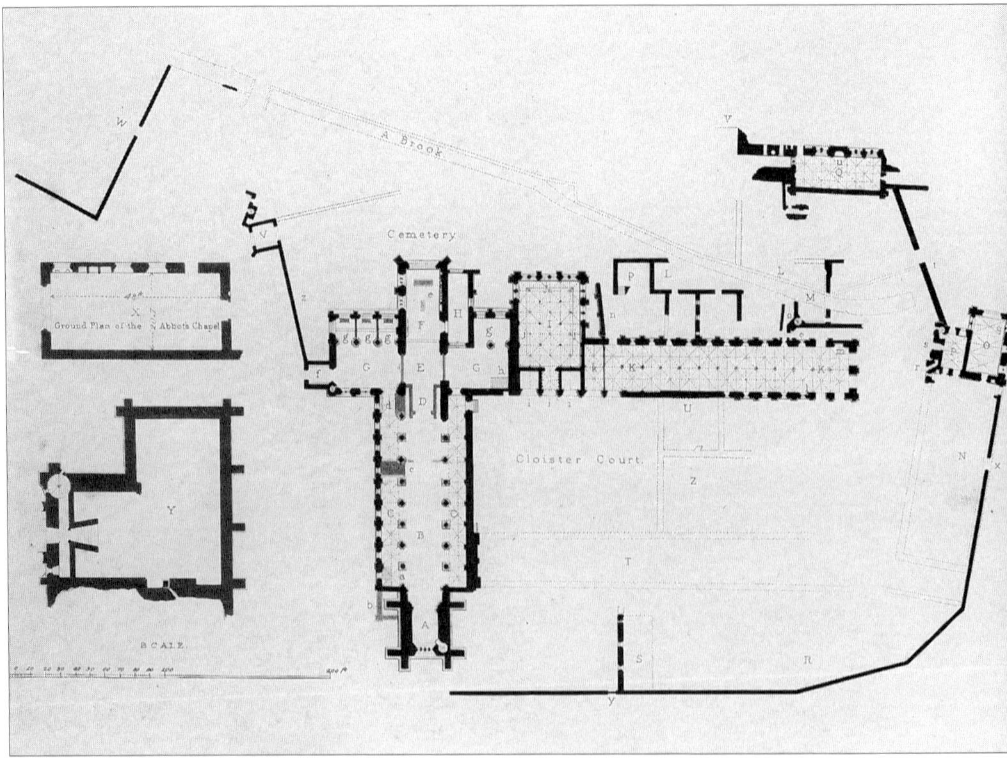

T. A. Beck, plan Furness Abbey, 1844. [Figure 2

compared, it is apparent that few of the measurements have been amended, indicating that West's accuracy was, for the most part, accepted (Figure 24).[24]

After his death, Close's notes were acquired and studied by Thomas Alcock Beck (1795–1846). Beck reorganised the manuscripts and went on to produce one of the foremost authoritative and scholarly works of the nineteenth century concerning Furness Abbey. The book, entitled *Annales Furnesienses*, was published in 1844 and was limited to 250 copies.[25] However, it has been consulted and cited many times since, and is still considered to be a very important piece of antiquarian research on the district of Furness. Close's last edition of West's work seems to have been superseded by Beck's more impressive publication on Furness Abbey and we note that, from 1859 to 1866, copies of the 1813 edition of Close's work were on sale by John Jackson of Ulverston for less than half the original price.[26]

A definite second stage in the way that ruined abbeys were viewed by the scholar now emerges. Excavation and clearing of the site were being undertaken and in-depth analysis of the architectural detail, and the dating of the surviving fabric, was being attempted. This development can be seen by a closer investigation of Beck's work.

Beck drew on many different sources, including extant documents and

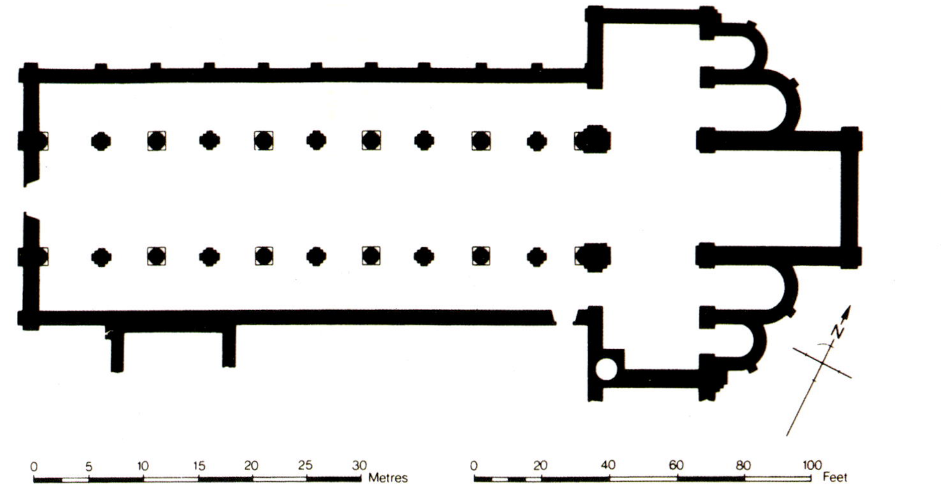

Plan of the church as first designed. The form of the east end of the presbytery at Furness is uncertain and the square end shown on the plan is based on the similar church at Vaux-de-Cernay in France

Plate 1. Plan of Furness Abbey Church, Dickinson/English Heritage, 1993.
(*Reproduced by permission of English Heritage*)

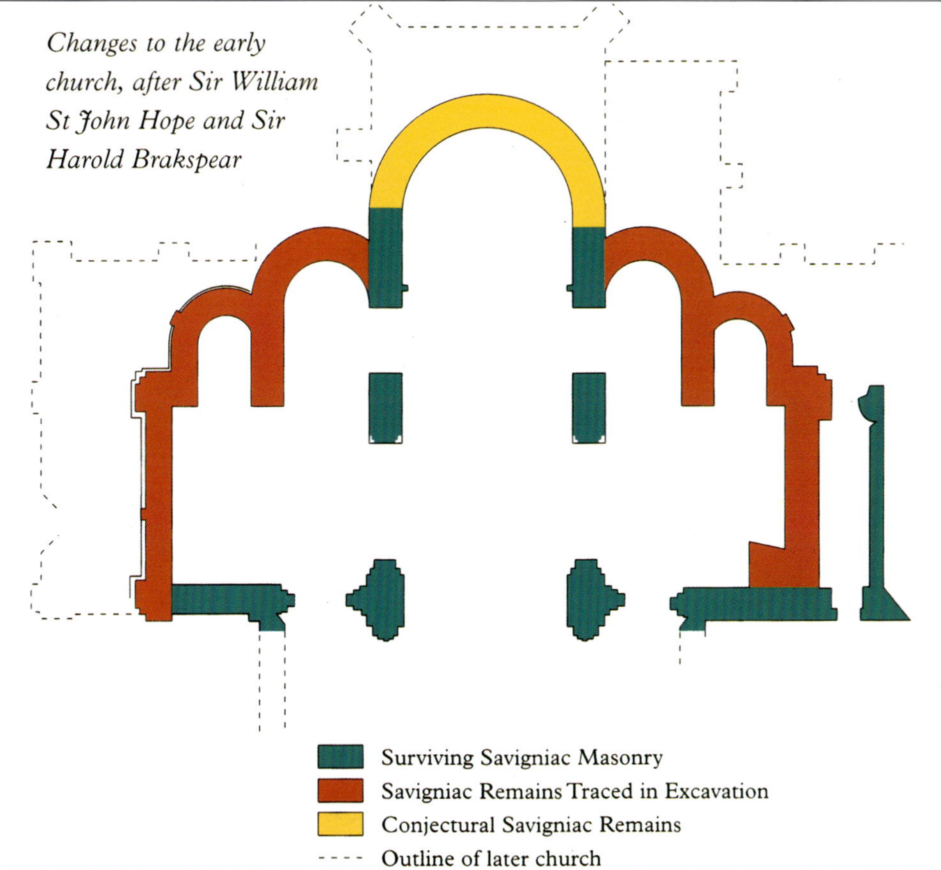

Plate 2. Plan of Furness Abbey Church, English Heritage, 1998.
(*Reproduced by permission of English Heritage*)

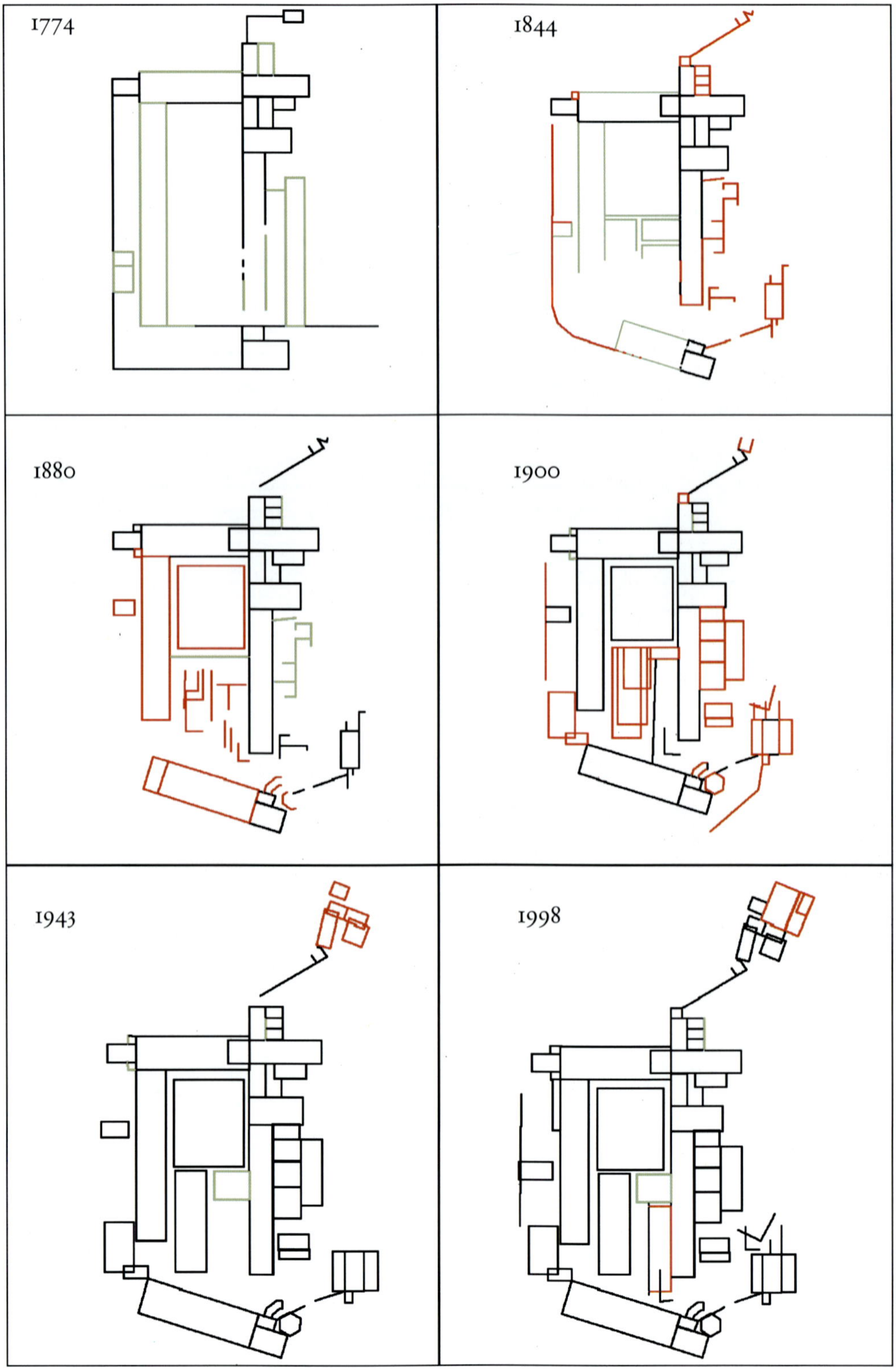
1774
1844
1880
1900
1943
1998

Plate 3 (*opposite*). Six representational plans of Furness Abbey.

Key to representational plans to illustrate significant finds of 'new' buildings on the Furness Abbey site over the past two hundred years.

Each box represents a building or room that was present on the previous or original plan.

Each box represents a building or room considered unimportant by the author or where the remains were not visible and their location has been estimated.

Each box represents a building or room that has been added since the previous plan.

Plan 1	T. West, *The Antiquities of Furness* (London, 1774).
Plan 2	T. A. Beck, *Annales Furnesienses: History and Antiquities of the Abbey of Furness* (London, 1844).
Plan 3	J. Richardson, *Furness, Past and Present: Its History and Antiquities*, vols. I–II (Barrow-in-Furness, 1880).
Plan 4	W. H. St John Hope, 'The Abbey of St Mary in Furness', *Transactions of the Cumberland and Westmorland Antiquarian and Archaeological Society*, xvi (1900).
Plan 5	S. J. Garton, *The Ancient Monuments and Historic Buildings: Furness Abbey* (London, 1943).
Plan 6	S. Harrison, J. Wood and R. Newman, *Furness Abbey, Cumbria* (London, 1998).

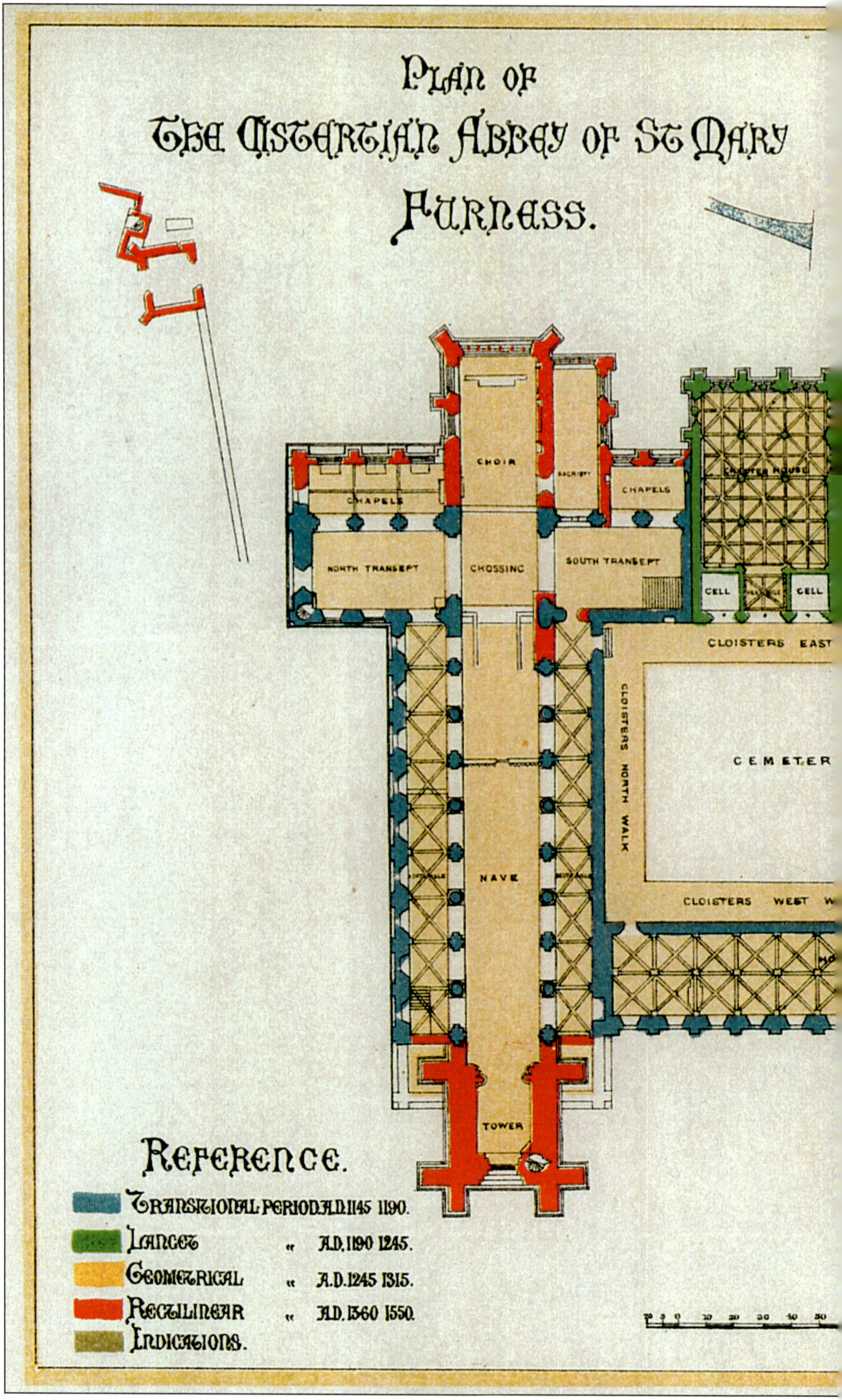
Plan of
The Cistertian Abbey of St Mary
Furness.
CHOIR
SACRISTY
CHAPELS
CHAPELS
CHAPTER HOUSE
NORTH TRANSEPT
CROSSING
SOUTH TRANSEPT
CELL
CELL
CLOISTERS EAST
CLOISTERS NORTH WALK
CEMETER
NAVE
CLOISTERS WEST W
TOWER
Reference.
Transitional Period A.D. 1145 1190.
Lancet " A.D. 1190 1245.
Geometrical " A.D. 1245 1315.
Rectilinear " A.D. 1360 1550.
Indications.

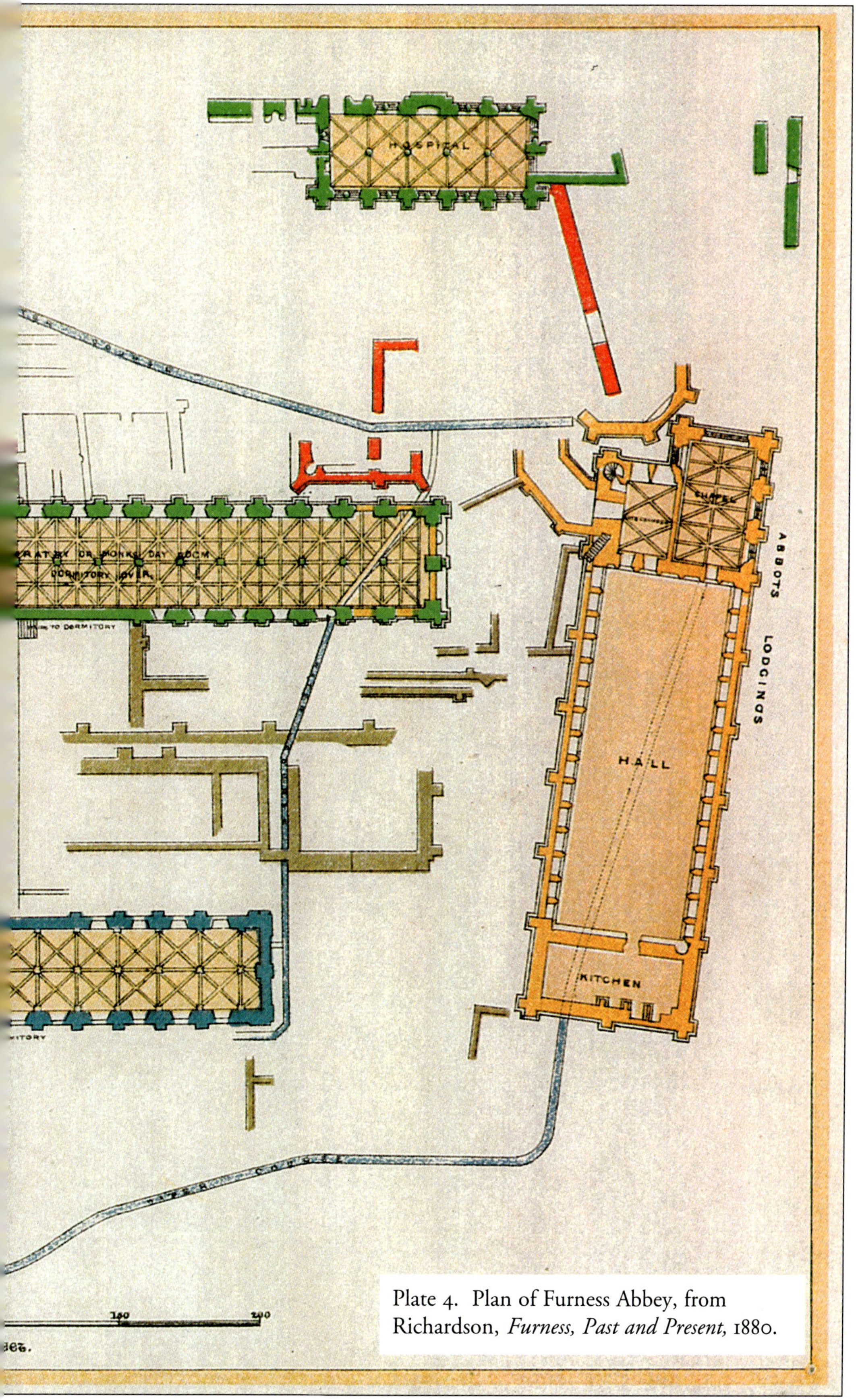

Plate 4. Plan of Furness Abbey, from Richardson, *Furness, Past and Present*, 1880.

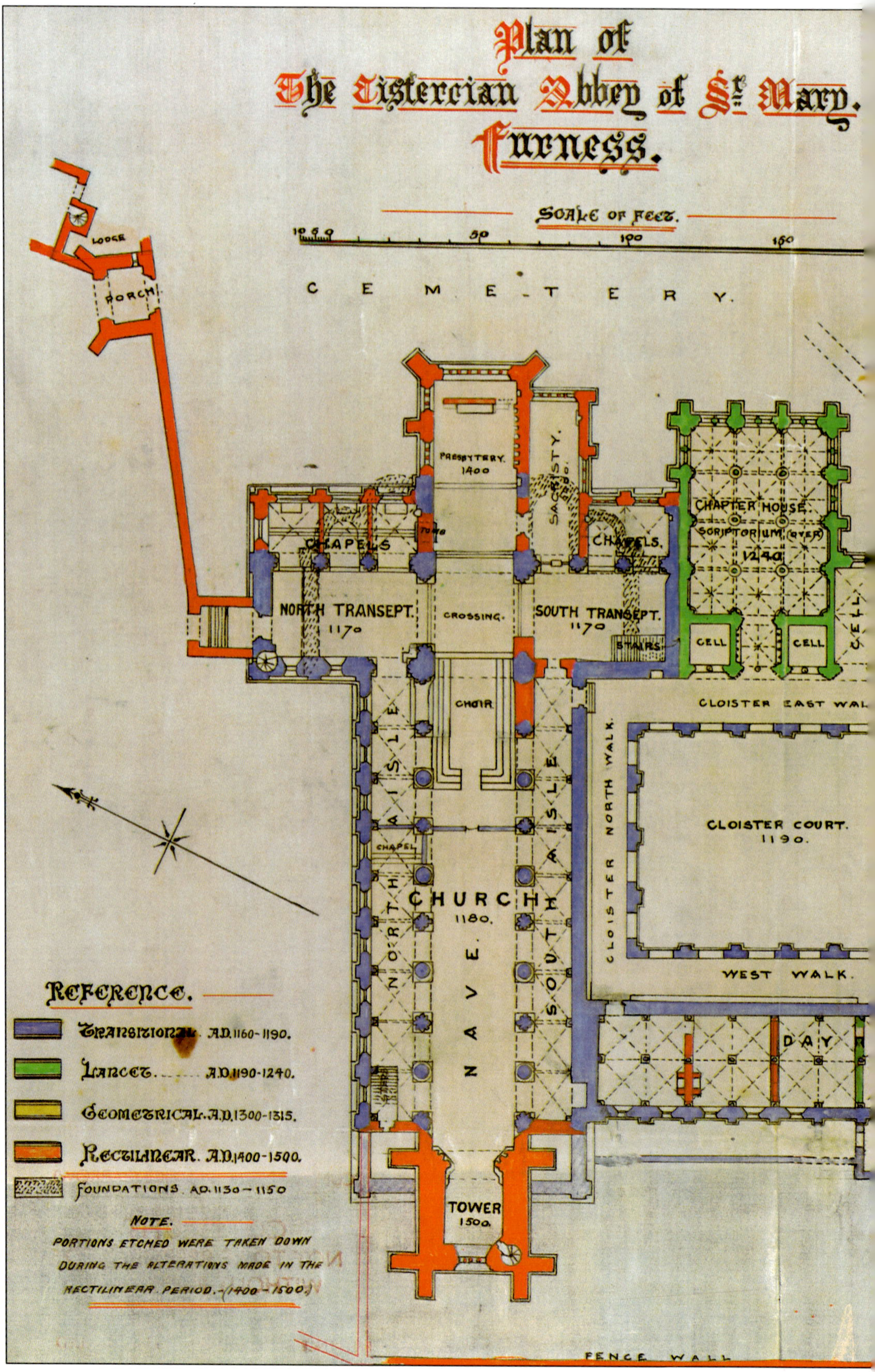

Plan of
The Cistercian Abbey of St. Mary.
Furness.
SCALE OF FEET.
10 5 0
50
100
150
CEMETERY.
LODGE
PORCH
PRESBYTERY.
1400
SACRISTY.
CHAPELS
TOMB
CHAPELS.
CHAPTER HOUSE.
SCRIPTORIUM (OVER)
1240
NORTH TRANSEPT.
1170
CROSSING.
SOUTH TRANSEPT.
1170
STAIRS
CELL
CELL
CELL
CHOIR
CLOISTER EAST WALK
CLOISTER NORTH WALK.
CLOISTER COURT.
1190.
NORTH AISLE
CHAPEL
CHURCH
1180.
NAVE.
SOUTH AISLE
WEST WALK.
DAY
REFERENCE.
Transitional. A.D.1160-1190.
Lancet. A.D.1190-1240.
Geometrical. A.D.1300-1315.
Rectilinear. A.D.1400-1500.
FOUNDATIONS. A.D.1130-1150
NOTE.
PORTIONS ETCHED WERE TAKEN DOWN DURING THE ALTERATIONS MADE IN THE RECTILINEAR PERIOD.-(1400-1500.)
TOWER
1500.
FENCE WALL

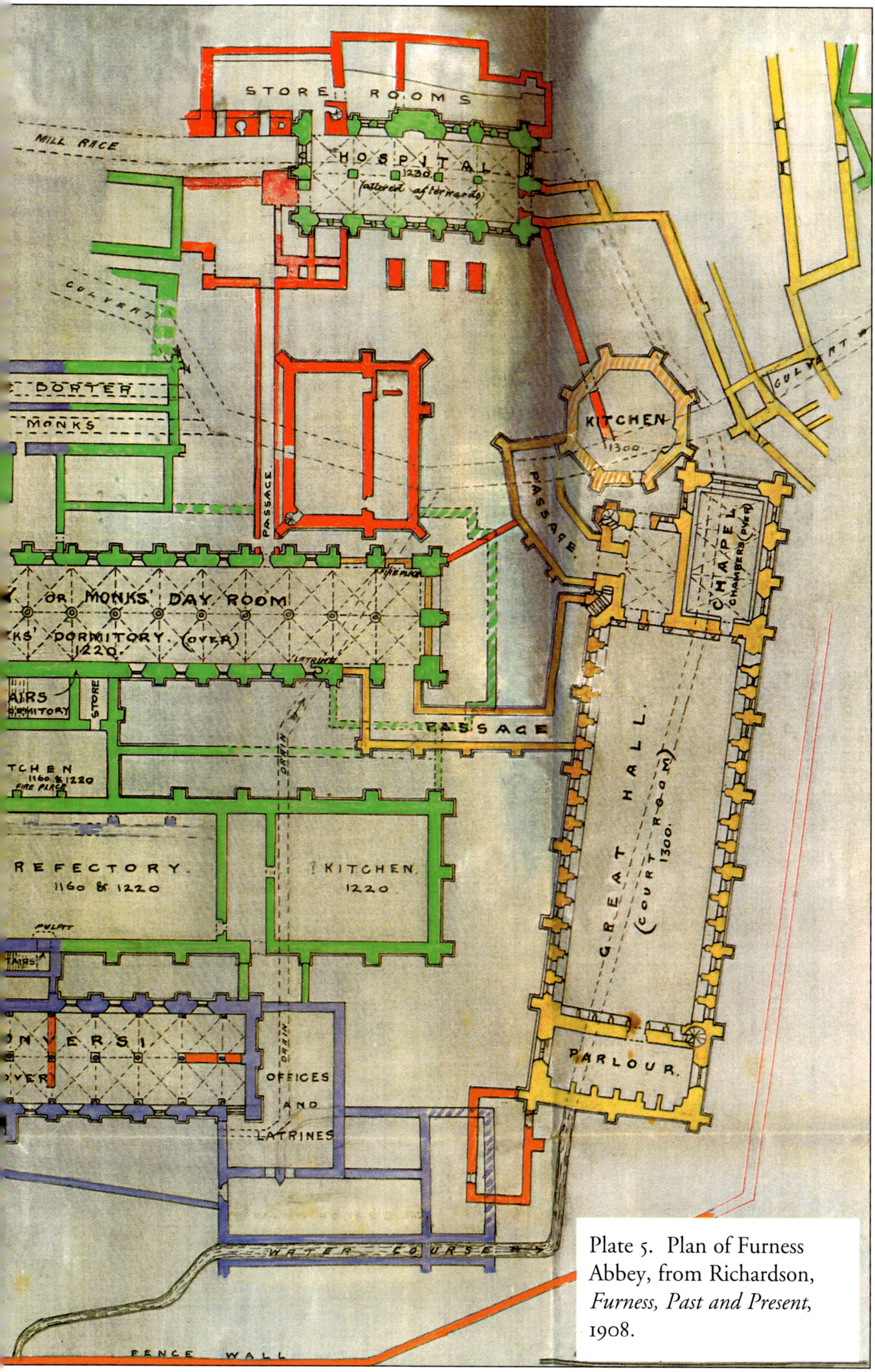

Plate 5. Plan of Furness Abbey, from Richardson, *Furness, Past and Present*, 1908.

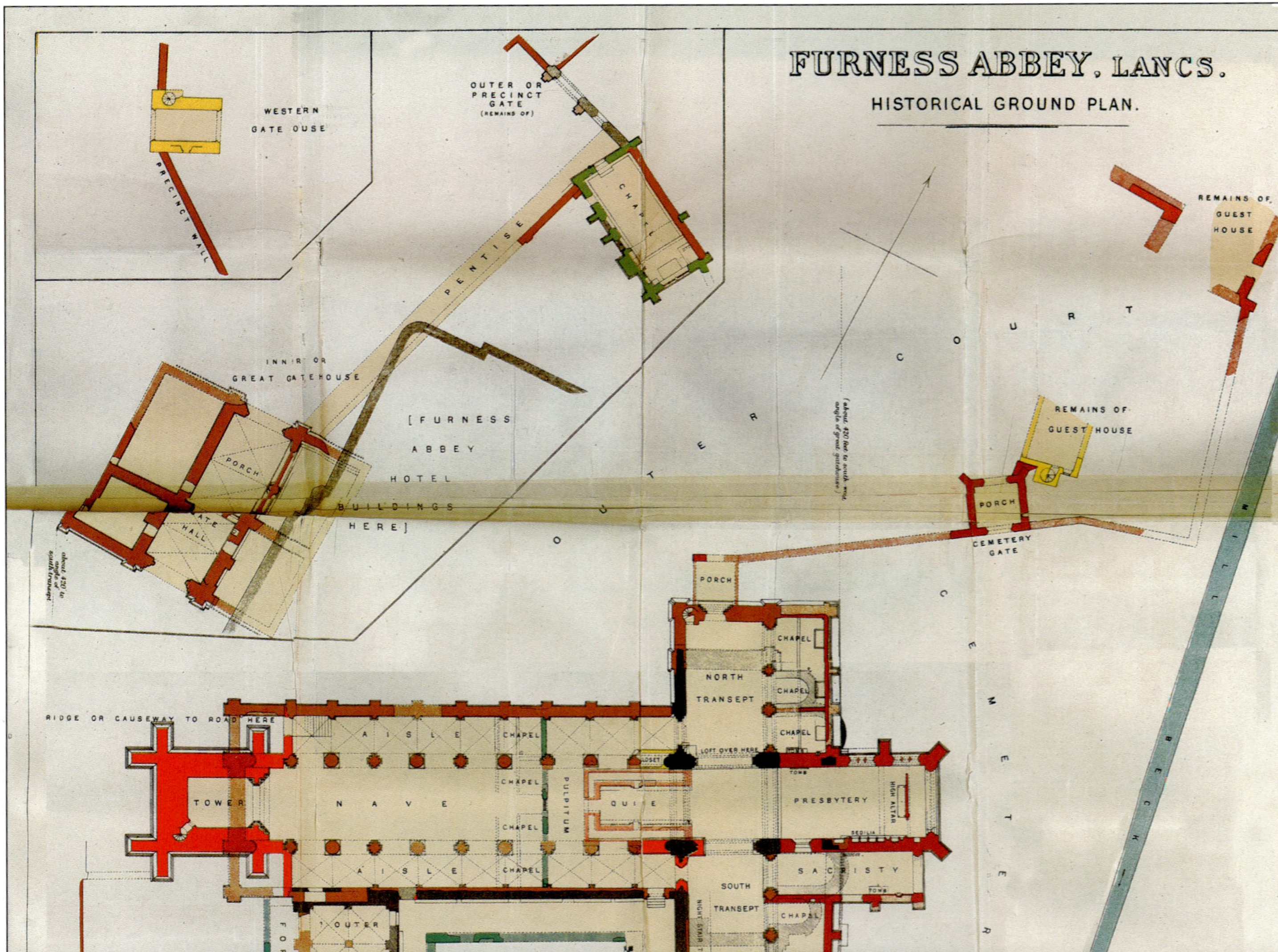
FURNESS ABBEY, LANCS.
HISTORICAL GROUND PLAN.
WESTERN GATE OUSE
PRECINCT WALL
OUTER OR PRECINCT GATE (REMAINS OF)
CHAPEL
PENTISE
INNIR OR GREAT GATEHOUSE
PORCH
GATE HALL
[FURNESS ABBEY HOTEL BUILDINGS HERE]
about 420 to angle of south transept
OUTER COURT
(about 420 feet to south-west angle of great gatehouse)
REMAINS OF GUEST HOUSE
REMAINS OF GUEST HOUSE
PORCH
CEMETERY GATE
MILL BECK
CEMETER
PORCH
NORTH TRANSEPT
CHAPEL
CHAPEL
CHAPEL
LOFT OVER HERE
RIDGE OR CAUSEWAY TO ROAD HERE
TOWER
AISLE
NAVE
AISLE
CHAPEL
CHAPEL
CHAPEL
CHAPEL
PULPITUM
QUIRE
PRESBYTERY
HIGH ALTAR
SEDILIA
TOMB
SACRISTY
TOMB
SOUTH TRANSEPT
NIGHT STAIR TO
CHAPEL
CHAPEL
OUTER
FOR

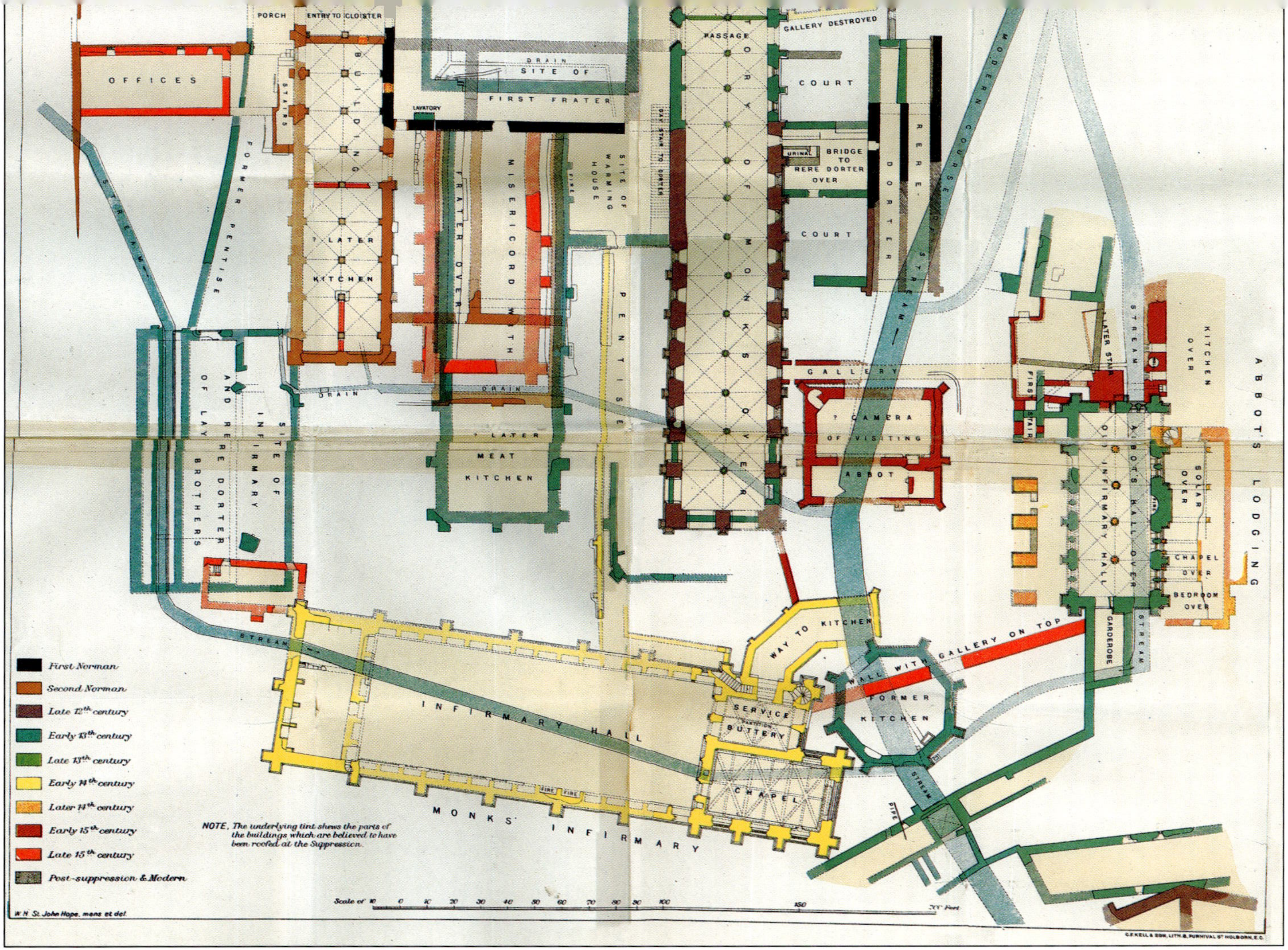

Plate 6.
Plan of
Furness
Abbey,
Hope,
c. 1900.
(*Reproduced
by permission
of CWAAS*)

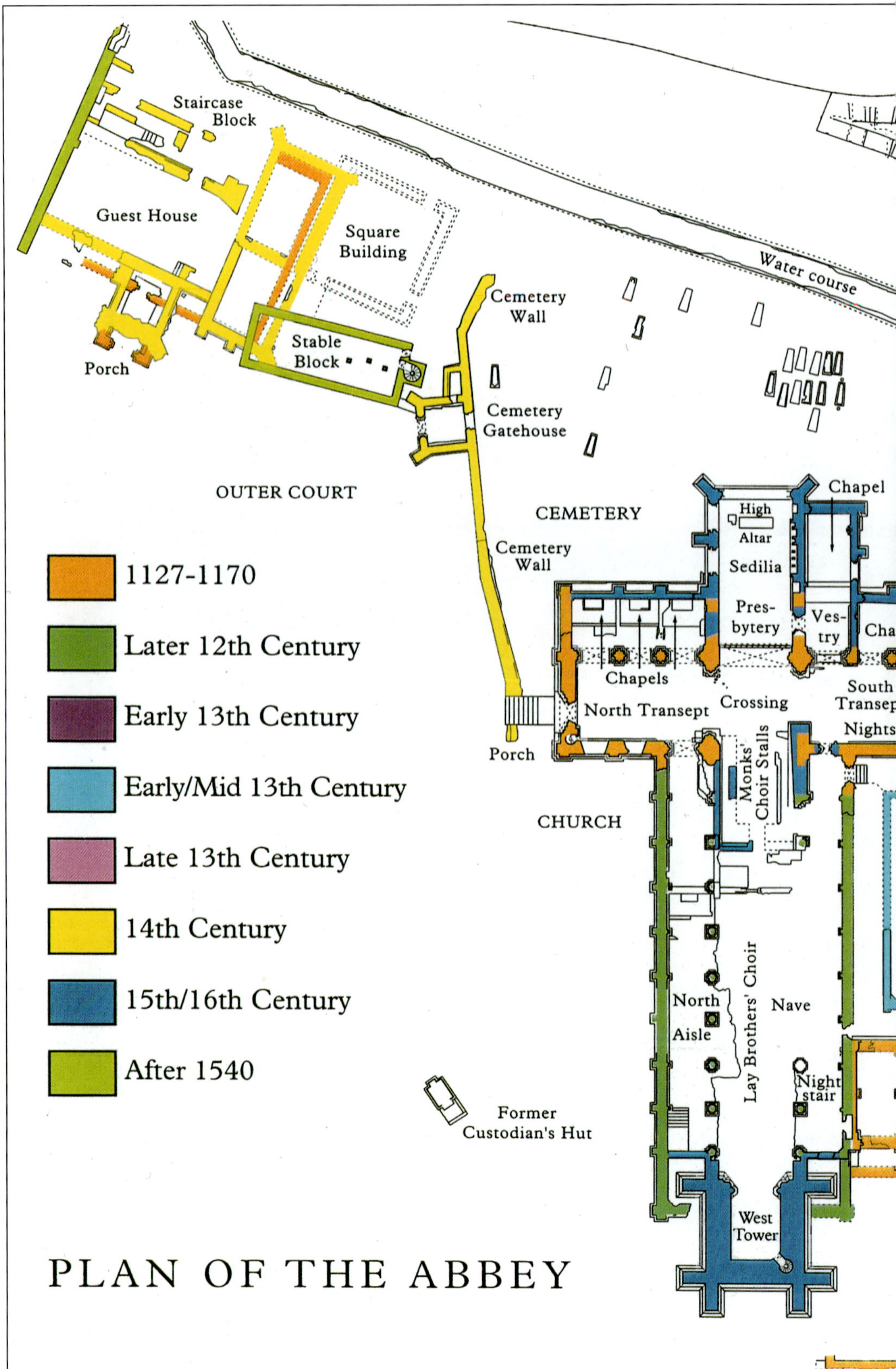

PLAN OF THE ABBEY

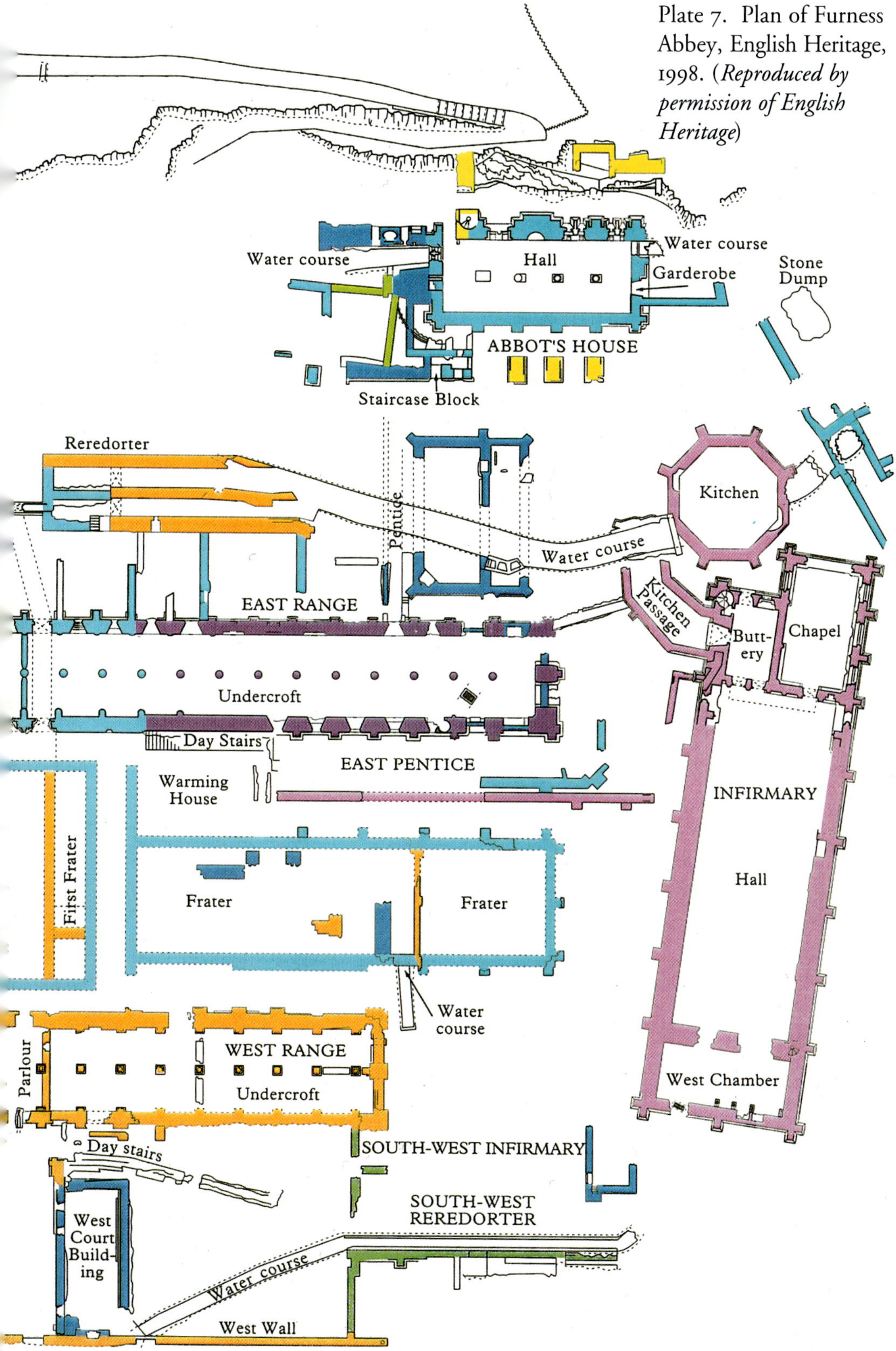

Plate 7. Plan of Furness Abbey, English Heritage, 1998. (*Reproduced by permission of English Heritage*)

Plate 8. Aerial photograph of Furness Abbey. (*Reproduced by permission of English Heritage*)

Plate 9. Map of Furness Abbey precinct, English Heritage, 1998.
(*Reproduced by permission of English Heritage*)

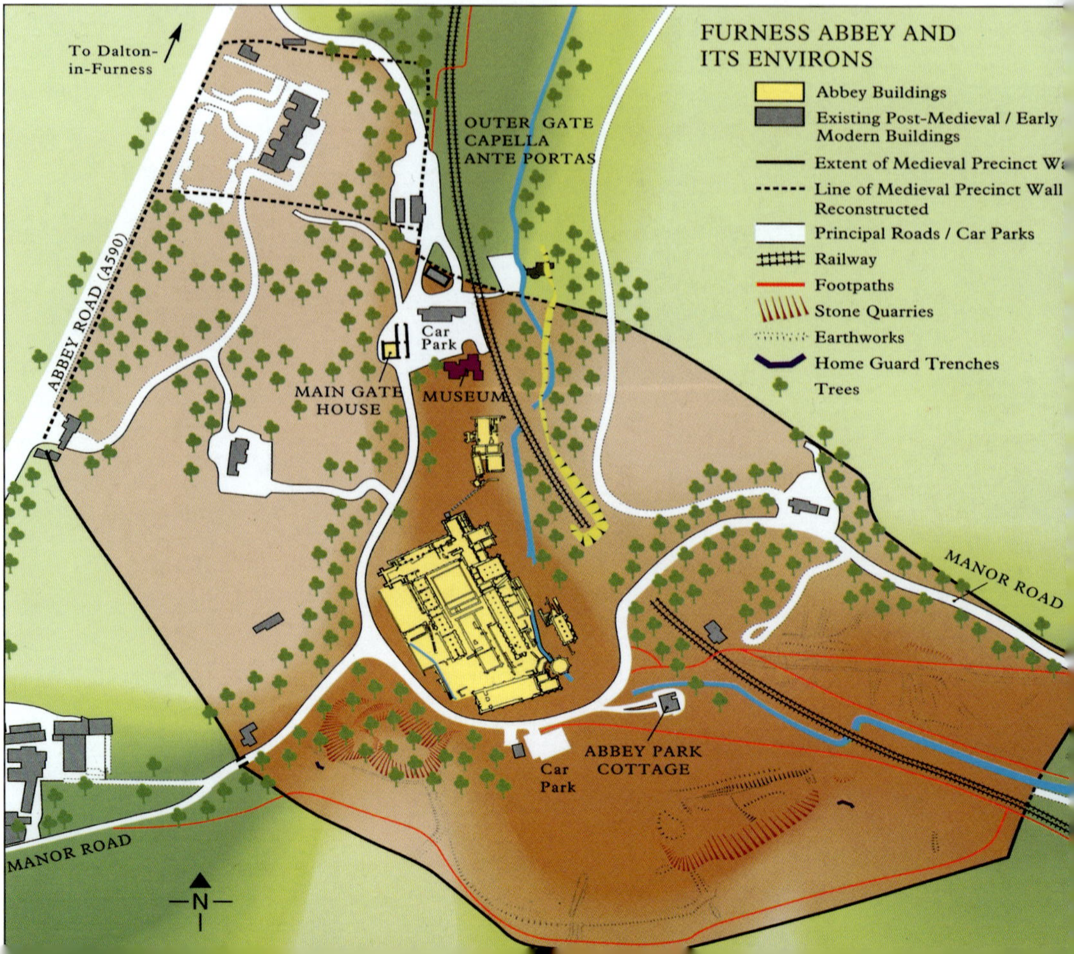

rness Abbey, the
ve arches in the
cloisters,
ıotograph, 1998.
[Figure 28]

other scholarly works, notably that of West. Attempts to clear some of the fallen masonry around the middle of the nineteenth century also revealed further evidence. Beck provided an integrated work, which included the history of the Cistercian Order, the history of the monastic community at Furness and a description of the ruins. The work also included many engravings, drawings, elevations and a new plan of the site, which is shown in Figure 27, and as the second of the six plans in Plate 3.[27]

Beck's plan, when compared to West's of 1774, differs in several respects. For example, the length of the cloister in West's work has been shortened by Beck. As this is represented by dotted lines it could indicate that Beck was not sure of his facts. However, Beck refers to the excavation 'lately' made in this area at the instigation of the Earl of Burlington. The cloister, he claims, was, as a consequence, full of rubbish which had been taken from other parts of the building.[28] The orientation of the infirmary hall (N) has been corrected, and the infirmary chapel has been correctly named (O). However, Beck seems to think it belonged to what he refers to as the guest hall (N), which he has outlined and which is a new addition since West's plan of 1774. Beck cites West's work and says that West had 'erroneously' denominated the chapel as a schoolroom.[29] The building beyond the watercourse has been marked, although Beck says that it is 'an apartment of indeterminate destination' (Q).[30] The long building on the south side of the chapter house is named as the 'common refectory', and more of the foundations are marked (K). Overall, Beck's tone is less presumptuous than West's when he seeks to identify buildings about which he is not entirely sure. When he does speculate, as for instance when he wonders if the guest hall may in fact be the infirmary, he is often right in his opinion although, as a cautious man, he admits that his work is open to error.[31] Beck is not afraid to argue against previous assertions, however. For example he states that West was wrong in his assumption that the stone used at Furness would not be suitable for any fine decorative work.[32]

Beck's work can be termed scholarly in many respects. His description of the buildings is very detailed and his drawings of the original carvinn-gs are impressive. A number of them have been included in this book as examples of Beck's own personal interpretation of the abbey ruins. One is an unattributed reconstruction of the chapter house doorway and vestibule shown in Figure 25.[33] The recent photograph of the same doorway shown in Figure 26 illustrates how detailed this reconstruction was. The artist has depicted the original detail of the mouldings, and Beck describes it as a 'multiplicity of concentric, plain mouldings'.[34] Figure 28 places the chapter house door as part of the row of five arches which, as we have seen in Chapter Two, have been the subject of many paintings.

Beck, when describing what he has attempted to show with these drawings, says that he has

> restor[ed] the groining of the chapter-room itself, insert[ed] glass in the windows and rubb[ed] a little of the rust of antiquity off the walls. The lower moulding of the arch could not be suitably restored and is therefore left on the plate as it exists in the original. A few monks are introduced to give an idea of height and perspective.[35]

Beck states that the engravings included in his book, are 'correct resemblances of the places they represent and not merely picturesque subjects made to please the artistic eye, though it will be admitted that most of the plates are truly picturesque notwithstanding'. In his observations, he displays an awareness of the penchant for the picturesque attributes of a ruin that existed during this period. He is also aware that Furness Abbey cannot compare with 'Bolton abbey as to picturesque effect, or with Fountains for architectural display, nor with Kirkstall or Rieval in a combination of both of these qualifications, yet its remains present a felicitous modification of them all'.[36] This work is clearly a scholarly analysis of Furness Abbey and has not been written for mere picturesque entertainment.

This is very evident in Beck's inclusion of extant documentary sources in his work. For example, he includes several facsimiles such as the signatures on the deeds of surrender, and several monastic arms. Beck's initial letter 'A' for three of his four chapters is a woodcut of the arms of Furness Abbey. In the same way, at the beginning of Chapter II he uses, as the initial letter 'T', a woodcut of the arms of Cîteaux Abbey. His work also contains several detailed architectural drawings that are a relatively true representation of the remains at the abbey. Figures 30 and 31 illustrate two of these drawings. Figure 30 is of a section through the chapter house stonework,[37] and Figure 31 is an elevation of the east end of the guest hall.[38] Nearly six decades later these two drawings were included in St John Hope's work *c.*1900, although the guest hall is relabelled 'Infirmary Chapel', a conclusion which still stands today. The two modern photographs alongside each drawing serve to illustrate just how accurate they were. If one looks closely at the photograph in

Above: Photograph of the chapter ouse wall, 1998. [Figure 29] *Right*: Section through the chapter house, 844. [Figure 30]

Figure 32, it will be seen that there is a fault on the stonework where the small tree was growing in the engraving found in Beck's work.

The stone carving of the elaborate sedilia at Furness Abbey is badly damaged today, and graffiti can be seen, some of which dates from the last century. Beck attempted to reconstruct the sedilia by the use of a drawing executed by H. Shaw and engraved by T. Turnbull. Beck also includes a description of the sedilia, a version of which is quoted in its entirety in a later and more accessible work: that of Richardson in 1880.[39]

Left: Section through the gue hall, 1844. [Figure 31]

Below: Photogra of the same vie 1998 [Figure 32

This drawing is shown in Figure 34,[40] whilst Figure 33 shows a recent photograph of the sedilia as it survives today. The visitor can find it in the south wall of the presbytery near the high altar beneath the east window. Beck's more detailed drawing of a section of the sedilia is illustrated in Figure 35, together with cross-sections of several bases shown with their ground lines and with details of the intricate carving of the corbels in the chancel.[41] All these drawings are intended to represent, as accurately as possible, the detail of the architecture.

p: Photograph of he sedilia, 1998. [Figure 33]

Bottom: econstruction of he sedilia, 1844. [Figure 34]

That Beck was aware of the need to preserve what remained of the sedilia is evident when he says that 'the Sedilia are well worthy of the most careful preservation by an enclosure of iron railing'.[42] However, the 'preservation' alluded to was, in fact, protection from further vandalism rather than further decay. When discussing the chapter house, however, Beck suggests that the vaulting of the ceiling, which was at that time lying on the floor of the building, could possibly be rescued and reconstructed.[43] In Chapter Two it was noted that a lot of this carved masonry was still lying on the ground at this time and it is possible that it was carted away either during the excavations at the end of the century or in the 1920s and 1930s, after the Office of Works took possession of the site.

On the dating of the surviving buildings, Beck concludes that

> it is impossible to state with precision at what periods the various edifices were commenced, renovated, altered or added to; the different styles of architecture alone are stepping stones by which to pass this chasm in the history of the Abbey and happily they are neither few nor far to seek.[44]

This indicates that Beck was aware that different architectural styles denoted different periods of construction. He was also knowledgeable about the fairly uniform plan adopted by the Cistercian Order and how this information could be used to advantage.[45] He also stated that, in order to assemble a complete plan of the site, 'heavy' excavations needed to be carried out.[46] His record of how Lord Cavendish ordered the inside of the west tower to be cleared reveals the drastic methods that were employed at this early date:

> the rubbish ... was rendered so compact by its fall, so tenacious by the rain, and was composed of such strongly cemented materials as to require blasting with gunpowder into manageable pieces for its removal.[47]

As stated, Beck included several paintings of the abbey in his work and an example, showing the west view of the transept, is reproduced in Figure 37.[48] This was incorporated as a double-page illustration. A modern photograph, again to show how accurate these architectural drawings were, despite the adornment of figures and animals, is shown in Figure 36.

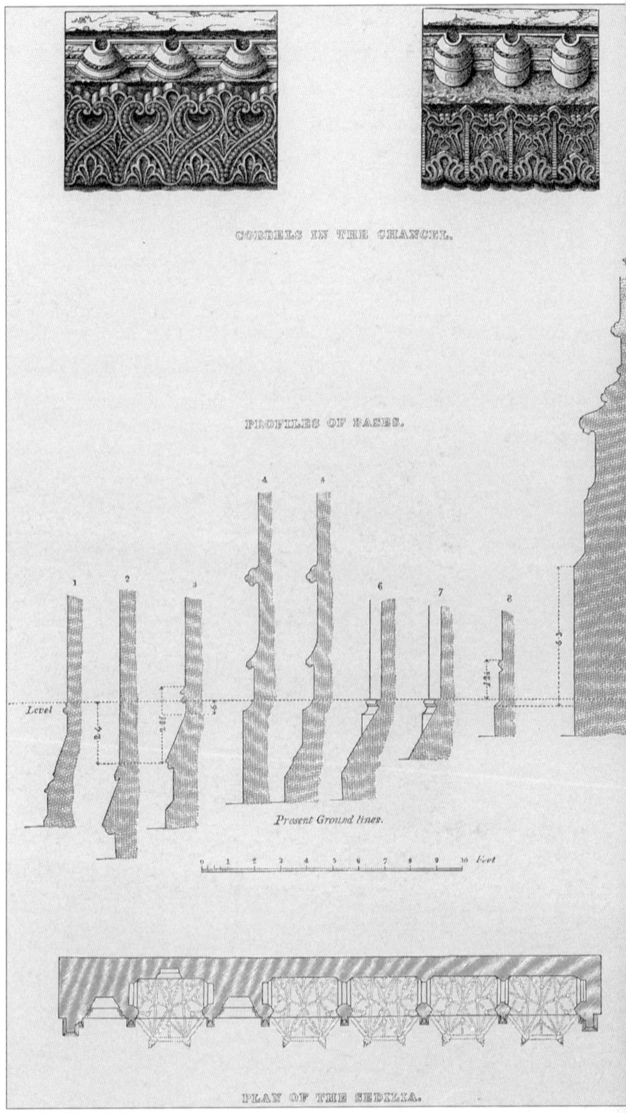

Detailed drawing of Furness Abbey 1844. [Figure 35]

Although Beck was more concerned with the main buildings of the monastery, he is not unaware of the existence of outer buildings in the precincts. He notes that there were once three mills, possibly obtaining this information from a close scrutiny of the cartulary.[49] He is, however, dismissive of the seventeenth-century manor house. This is also true of many of the antiquarians of this period who had little interest in the post-Dissolution buildings.[50]

Beck's concern regarding the railway which was about to be constructed (Beck is writing in 1842), is worth quoting in full as it provides an additional motive for his own recordings: to preserve the ruins by the use of the pen rather than by more physical means.

> but when the report … that a fumiferous railroad is about to desecrate with its horrisonous traffic even this peaceful, this solitary vale, and to tear away all that the hoary-headed has spared so long, – it may be allowed to linger over an attempt to perpetuate these memorials of long by-gone days by a somewhat lengthened description.[51]

Beck's work was scholarly, well documented and well researched and improved substantially on the work executed by West half a century earlier. Within two decades of the publication of Beck's work, other historians were conducting tours around the ruins in order to spread the

ht: Photograph the west view ̄ the transept,)8. [Figure 36]

low: Engraving the same view, 14. [Figure 37]

knowledge. For example, in 1868 the eminent Lancaster architect and historian Edmund Sharpe (1808–77) took some members from the Royal Archaeological Institute of Great Britain and Ireland round the abbey. The itinerary for that day has been preserved in a printed guidebook and this is shown in Figure 38.[52] There is an attempt to date the buildings which, together with the indication in the title that this was a tour concerned with the architectural history of the abbey, is a good example of the importance that was placed, at this time, on the history of the buildings rather than of monasticism. Sharpe's great interest in Romanesque and Gothic architecture of the Middle Ages is reflected in the many churches that were built from his designs during the period 1836 to 1851. His published books and articles earned him the reputation of being an authority on Cistercian abbeys and he was often called upon to conduct guided tours.[53]

Further developments in the evolution of the scholarly study of monastic remains can be gleaned from the several editions of Joseph Richardson's work, *Furness, Past and Present.* This was first published in the 1872 and its data on Furness Abbey were largely taken from Beck's work, thus indicating that it was Beck, not West, who was now considered the authority on the remains of the abbey.

The plan contained in the 1880 edition of this work is shown as the third plan in Plate 3, and in Plate 4.[54] What is immediately apparent is that it is in colour, with each colour representing the period when the surviving section of masonry was assumed to have been erected. The realisation that details of other periods of construction could be gleaned from a study of the existing fabric was becoming apparent and, as excavation was carried out in a more systematic way, the plans in subsequent editions of Richardson's work were altered to reflect this new knowledge.

Plate 5 reproduces the plan from Richardson's 1908 edition based on a plan executed in 1900 by St John Hope. One very obvious difference is that the cloister court was named as the cemetery in 1880 and, in the 1908 version, this has been corrected. There is very little speculation here; the walls are shown, not as dotted lines, but as existing substantial remains. Part of the octagonal kitchen is shown for the first time and the later edition completes and names it. The 1908 version also names many of the buildings on the south side of the cloister which are only outlined in the 1880 plan, and Richardson is very definite about naming the monks reredorter behind the chapter house.

In Richardson's own words, the motive for the publication of his work was that:

> The former histories of Furness have long been out of print, and the immense development of the mineral wealth of the district, during the last few years, has made the Furness of the present time, in many

> respects, widely different from what it was in the days of West or of Close or even of the late Edward Baines.[55]

The scholarly aspect of Richardson's work is very apparent. Indeed he is very vocal in his views on the 'Picturesque and Romantic' movement. He sings the praises of the medieval architects, or masons, and damns the 'second-rate painters and third-rate poets [who] have been able to win immortality' whilst 'men to whose genius we are indebted for our noble abbeys and cathedrals have been allowed to sink into the nameless grave'.[56] However, he is not averse to quoting some poetry himself, notably a poem by Bryant called *The Knight's Epitaph*.[57] He includes this in his description of the two helmeted effigies which were found in the church nave and removed to the infirmary chapel.

The dating of these effigies, together with two others which were found in the north aisle, could only be guessed at. All four were incorporated as very detailed drawings in Beck's work of 1844. These drawings are shown in Figure 39.[58] The accuracy of these drawings clearly identifies them as scholarly works. The effigies have now been restored by English Heritage and are displayed in the small museum at the visitor centre.

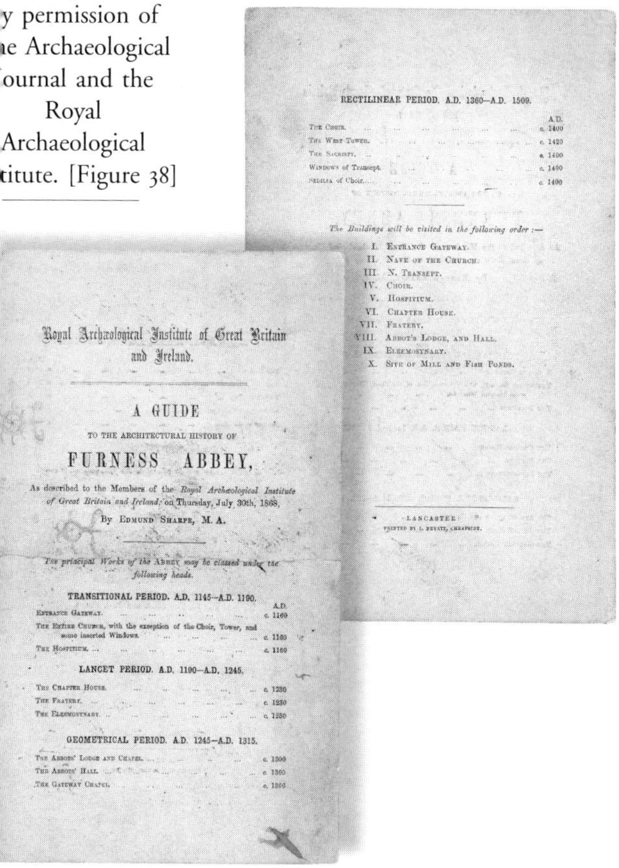

Royal Archæological Institute of Great Britain and Ireland.

A GUIDE

TO THE ARCHITECTURAL HISTORY OF

FURNESS ABBEY,

As described to the Members of the *Royal Archæological Institute of Great Britain and Ireland*, on Thursday, July 30th, 1868,

By Edmund Sharpe, M. A.

The principal Works of the Abbey *may be classed under the following heads.*

TRANSITIONAL PERIOD. A.D. 1145–A.D. 1190.

	A.D.
Entrance Gateway.	c. 1160
The Entire Church, with the exception of the Choir, Tower, and some inserted Windows	c. 1160
The Hospitium.	c. 1160

LANCET PERIOD. A.D. 1190–A.D. 1245.

The Chapter House.	c. 1230
The Fratery.	c. 1230
The Eleemosynary.	c. 1230

GEOMETRICAL PERIOD. A.D. 1245–A.D. 1315.

The Abbots' Lodge and Chapel	c. 1300
The Abbots' Hall.	c. 1300
The Gateway Chapel.	c. 1300

RECTILINEAR PERIOD. A.D. 1360–A.D. 1509.

	A.D.
The Choir.	c. 1400
The West Tower.	c. 1420
The Sacristy.	c. 1400
Windows of Transept.	c. 1400
Sedilia of Choir.	c. 1400

The Buildings will be visited in the following order:—

I. Entrance Gateway.
II. Nave of the Church.
III. N. Transept.
IV. Choir.
V. Hospitium.
VI. Chapter House.
VII. Fratery.
VIII. Abbot's Lodge, and Hall.
IX. Eleemosynary.
X. Site of Mill and Fish Ponds.

LANCASTER:
PRINTED BY I. BRYATT, CHEAPSIDE.

:mund Sharpe, *A Guide to the ·hitectural History f Furness Abbey,* 68. Reproduced y permission of ie Archaeological ournal and the Royal Archaeological titute. [Figure 38]

Richardson's early twentieth-century plan in Plate 5 was clearly influenced by the work of Sir William H. St John Hope (1854–1919). Hope was an antiquary and archaeologist and wrote numerous ecclesiological and heraldic works. His interest in Furness Abbey stretched over many years and included extensive excavations. Although various clearances had taken place in the grounds of the abbey during the nineteenth century, little work had been done to excavate the remains below the surface, and this Hope redressed at the end of the century.

Hope's plan of 1900 is shown as the fourth plan in Plate 3 and a scaled down version can be seen in Plate 6. The original measured approximately twenty inches by thirty-two inches.[59] Hope's ground plan was published to accompany his article in the *Transactions of the Cumberland and Westmorland Antiquarian and Archaeological Society* in 1900, and this large plan was folded and placed at the back of the volume.[60] In drawing this plan, Hope collaborated with two contemporaries, the architects Sir Harold Brakspear (1870–1934) and Sir Charles Reed Peers (1868–1952). Peers became the Chief Inspector of Ancient Monuments at the Office of Works (1910–33) and was heavily involved in defining the principles of architectural conservation. The Ancient Monuments Act of 1911 enabled the State to take into its care many ruins of archaeological and architectural importance. Peers was involved with many of these sites, including Furness Abbey, continuing the work of Hope and Brakspear.

Hope's excavation at Furness Abbey was primarily to uncover the ground plan. His method was to use trial trenches to find the foundations and then, by scientific observation, to establish where the foundations began and ended. Although these methods tended to be destructive, particularly of the archaeological stratification, they proved to be effective and reasonably reliable. Writing in 1990, G. Coppack, whilst recognising the value of Hope's work, says of his excavation technique that he possessed a 'quick method of recovering ground plans [but] it did untold damage to archaeological deposits that post-dated the construction of individual walls'.[61]

The use of colour to indicate the age of the standing masonry and the identification of further buildings was a feature of Hope's later plans. This was

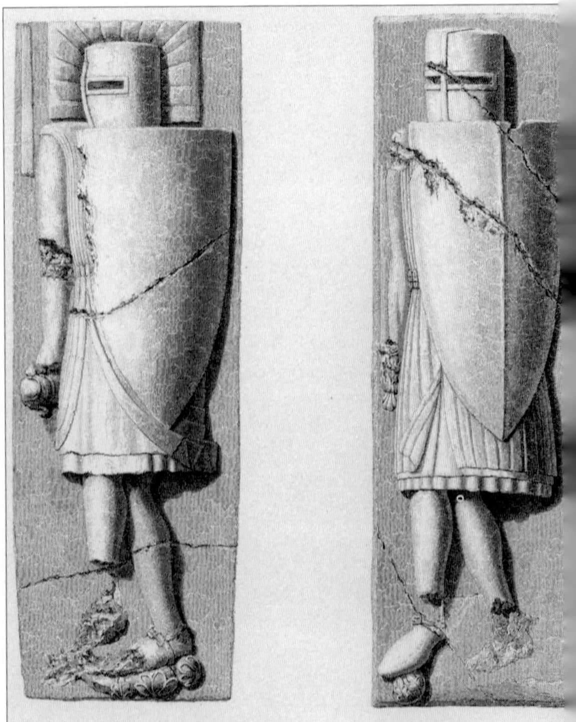

Effigies found in Furness Abbey. [Figure 39]

as a direct result of Hope's own archaeological excavations that were begun in September 1896 and continued in the autumn months of 1897 and 1898. These excavations were arranged by the CWAAS after permission had been obtained from the owner of the site, Victor Cavendish.

Hope's findings on Furness were published in the 1900 journal of the CWAAS and were later reproduced as a separate book in 1902. Both publications included a general history of Furness Abbey and its architectural history, together with details of the site and precinct including two spliced drawings, twelve black and white photographs of the buildings, a plan of the precinct (Figure 40), the large folded plan and the Curwen elevation of the presbytery (Figure 41). Also included are eight drawings, most of which were copied from Beck's 1844 work.[62]

Hope claims that Beck was responsible for clearing the church and 'other parts' of rubble approximately sixty years earlier, but the cloister and other monastic buildings were cleared in 1881–2 under 'the superintendence of Mr W. B. Kendall'.[63] Hope also states that, at this time, the buildings were 'freed from ivy and other parasitical vegetation by the direction of Lord Frederick Cavendish before he died in 1882'.[64] The word 'parasitical' indicates that, by the late nineteenth century, the 'picturesque' vegetation was now viewed as a direct threat to the surviving buildings.

Separately shown on Hope's ground plan and reproduced in Plate 6, is the Furness Abbey Hotel which was built on the site of the old seventeenth-century manor house. Hope, however, largely ignored these post-Dissolution buildings. He focused on the church, cloister buildings and gatehouse and there was no attempt to locate the other precinct buildings that were recorded in contemporary documentary evidence.

A publication of 1902 mentions Hope's recent article in the CWAAS and credits him with the finding of many unearthed foundations, including the apses of chapels in the transepts of the original Norman church and the octagonal kitchen.[65] This can be clearly seen on his plan in Plate 6. Hope has also added outlines of many of the foundations of the claustral buildings and has identified a number of these buildings, including the infirmary hall, formerly known as the great hall. He also identifies the abbots' lodgings on the east of the site, from which he says he had excavated a large amount of soil.[66] An elevation of the north side of the presbytery is included in his work and is shown in Figure 41. Hope attributes these drawings to Mr John F. Curwen.[67] These very detailed elevations, which were printed in colour, were thought to be important enough to warrant a double page foldout, indicative of the scholarly aspect of Hope's work.

Hope was still excavating after 1900, and many of his notes and writings have still to be interpreted and published. His published work, for example, lacks trench plans and detailed records of other artefacts found. Hope worked closely with Harold Brakspear, but Fergusson highlights the fact that Hope and Brakspear 'posit opposed construction sequences'.[68]

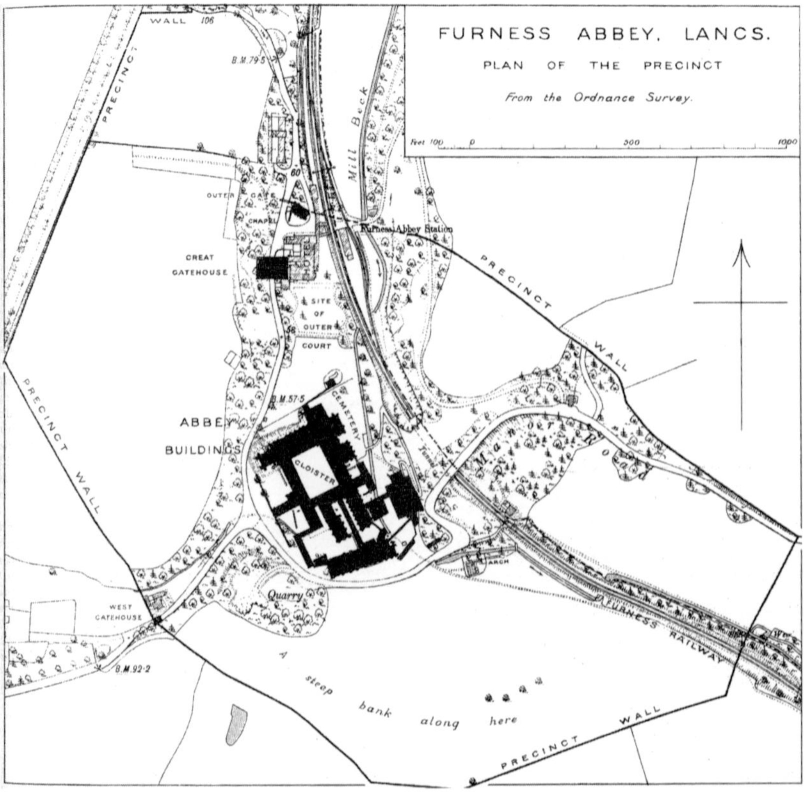

Plan of Furness Abbey precinct c.1900. Reproduc[ed] by permission [of] CWAAS. [Figure 40]

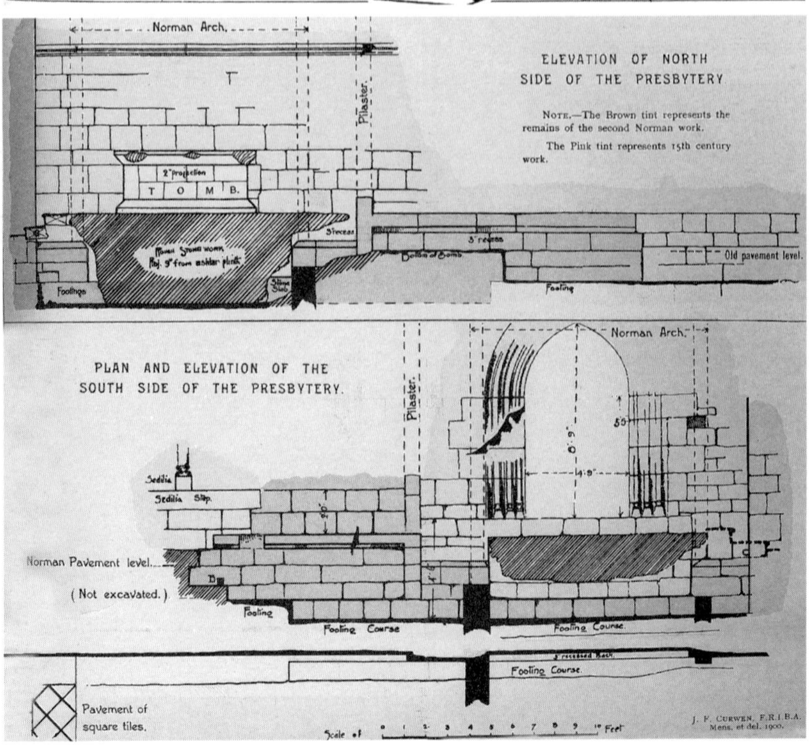

Elevation of th[e] north and sout[h] side of the presbytery. Reproduced by permission of CWAAS. [Figure

Furness is a complicated site and the damage done by the Dissolution and subsequent use of the site as a quarry, compounded by neglect, made the interpretation of the ruins difficult. Moreover Fergusson maintains that, as early as the fifteenth century, alterations to the fabric of the buildings, including the western tower, had destroyed much of the earlier structures.[69]

However, archaeological methods were slowly developing and Brakspear started to concentrate on the monastic precinct as a whole. Moreover, instead of relying entirely on trenching to recover walls, he began to use area excavation. Brakspear was also beginning to realise that early buildings were not always untraceable, as excavation can sometimes reveal evidence below the surviving buildings. Coppack credits Brakspear's monastic plans, though not specifically those of Furness Abbey, with 'including little in the way of supposition – a distinct improvement on the work of Hope'.[70]

Brakspear had disagreed with Hope about the interpretation of the east end of the church and in 1900 he wrote an article in the *Transactions of the Lancashire and Cheshire Antiquarian Society* about the first Savignac church at Furness Abbey.[71] Brakspear admits that there is little known about the Savignac churches due to the fact that these early buildings have all been altered since 1148, being replanned on the Cistercian style. Brakspear compared Furness with the Abbey of Vaux de Cernay in Paris, another Savignac house colonised in 1118, and, with the aid of diagrams, he offers the suggestion that the earlier church at Furness was of a similar design.[72] Brakspear's claim that there is evidence of the Savignac church beneath the existing remains has subsequently been proved correct.

By this time the need to preserve monastic remains was also beginning to be recognised. The fabric of Furness Abbey had previously been quarried for its stone, lead and timber, the loss of which created the ruin. According to Richardson, the Commissioners of Henry VIII, a few years after the Dissolution, removed 'a quantity of the debris ... for the purpose of repairing Dalton Castle'.[73] Paul Kelly confirmed this in his article of 1929. He also described the ruinous state of the castle and tells us that 'in ... 1546, William Sandes, the Kings Bailiff, was ordered to proceed with the immediate repair of the castle'.[74]

By the mid-nineteenth century, the writer, John Ruskin (1819–1900), was becoming alarmed at the number of national monuments that were in danger of being demolished or restored without due regard for their intrinsic value as historical documents. He stated in his book, *The Seven Lamps of Architecture*, that, on the question of whether we should endeavour to preserve our historic monuments, 'we have no right whatever to touch them. They are not ours. They belong partly to those who built them, and partly to all the generations of mankind who are to follow us.'[75] This concern, which was shared by others, including the poet and craftsman, William Morris (1834–96) led to the establishment, in 1877, of the Society for the Protection of Ancient Buildings.

An insight into the philosophy of this Society can be gleaned from *Notes on the Repairs of Ancient Buildings*, written in 1903, where it was stated that:

> The conditions and surroundings of every period are different, so that the motives which act on men of one age cannot govern the productions of genuine work conceived in the spirit and embodied in the forms of another ... Even were it possible to reproduce lost work, it may be said that in matters artistic honesty is the best policy, just as much as in other affairs of life. The restorer is in reality committing a forgery.[76]

By 1910, when Charles Peers was appointed as the Ancient Monuments Inspector, there were eighty-nine monuments in State care including many medieval buildings and ruins. Peers's appointment heralded a new era in the history of the care of ancient monuments, particularly in respect of the protection and repair of ruins.

The various government departments concerned have, through legislation and state funding, been responsible for preserving many ruins. The work and history of the Ministry of Works is outlined in *The Ministry of Works*, written by Sir Harold Emmerson, formerly Permanent Secretary of the Ministry. He particularly focused on the State as a guardian of the past, and on how the buildings in its care were preserved. He states that 'generally no attempt [is made] at restoration to its original form, and work is confined as far as possible to the preservation of existing remains'.[77]

The initial excavations following the establishment of the Office of Works in 1913, were not only concerned with the clearance of sites in order to preserve them, but also with displaying them for public consumption.[78] Archaeological stratification was, however, still largely ignored, although the need to preserve and display incidentally revealed further information about the hidden structures. The 'plan' did, however, take precedence over the detailed elevation and section drawings that can be seen in Beck's and Hope's work.

Furness Abbey was transferred to the guardianship of the Office of Works in 1923, as were many medieval ruins. J. C. Dickinson, the author of a sequence of reprints of the Ministry of Works guides, published over several decades after the Second World War, states that although excavations were made (*c.*1920s) 'in connection with the repair of the church and chapter house ... reports of work [have] not survived'. Dickinson maintained that the only account of these excavations in print was the brief report of Sir Charles Peers's address in a CWAAS publication of 1928.[79] Jason Wood however states that there is a substantial amount of material dating from the 1920s contained in the unpublished project archive compiled by Lancaster University Archaeological Unit staff. This archive contains around 50 early excavation records including a substantial archive of St John Hope's unpublished excavations.[80]

The remedial work carried out in the 1920s included concrete underpinning in the north transept and the chapter house. A clearer understanding of the problems connected with medieval foundations has been gained by this necessary preservation work. Dickinson also wrote that, *c.*1946, at the suggestion of Mr J. L. Hobbs, 'a small excavation was made ... which revealed well worked octagonal bases at least a foot below the present level'.[81] In this article Dickinson also 'corrected' several of Hope's observations and referred to another excavation undertaken in 1925, giving details of what it revealed.

The ground plan of 1943, shown as the fifth image in Plate 3, and in Figure 42, was drawn when Furness Abbey had been under State control for twenty years. The Ministry of Works published this plan as a centre spread in a booklet, written by S. J. Garton, that is described as a 'short guide'. The booklet states that the 'plan will be found adequate to illustrate the text'. This publication includes brief historical notes, but mainly consists of a descriptive tour of Furness Abbey.[82] It should be noted that the plan is a simplified version of Hope's plan, but was not necessarily aimed at an academic audience. No key is given, although the text does attempt to date the buildings. The abbot's lodging is shown as a more complete building and named correctly, and, by the addition of 'open' lines, the guesthouse has been highlighted to the north east of the church. A custodian's hut to the south west of the plan is also included together with arrows that direct the visitor from the hut, which is at the entrance to the site, into the nave of the Church. Further arrows point the way to the railway station. This is indicative of the development of guidebooks for the use of the casual visitor rather than as scholarly works.

Dickinson also showed an interest in the site of the Manor House and the later Furness Abbey Hotel. He corrected the 'ancient guide-books' in their belief that the abbot's house once stood on this site and relocated it to the position where it is marked on modern plans. He also lamented the loss of the hotel before any survey could be undertaken, although he did state that he visited the site whilst the building was being demolished and he saw nothing 'clearly of medieval or even pre-Victorian date'.[83] This may indicate that his focus was still on the medieval buildings rather than encompassing the whole history of the site, including the post-Dissolution buildings.

During the early years when the site was under the guardianship of the Ministry of Works, little additional information on Furness Abbey was revealed. However, by the 1960s, excavation was increasingly focused on the other features to be found in the monastic precinct, and, by the 1970s, interest in other aspects, such as the economy of a monastery, was developing. This resulted in a multidimensional recording of monasticism

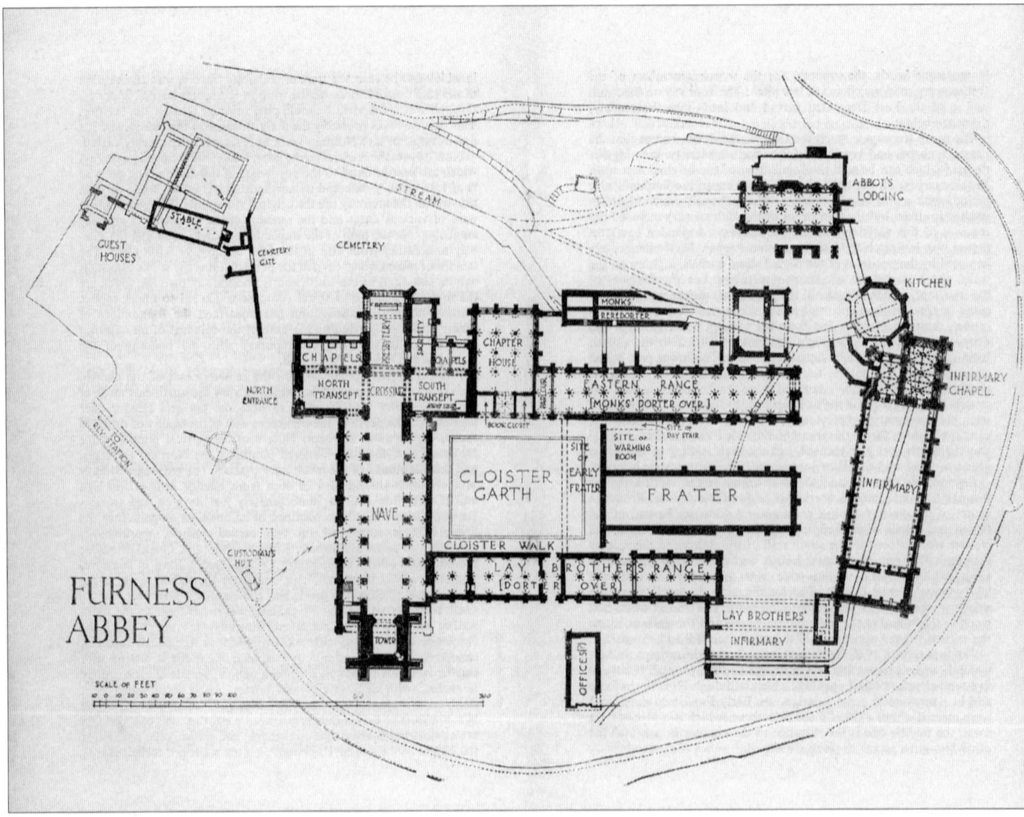

S. J. Garton, plan of Furness Abbey 1943. Reproduced by permission of English Heritage. [Figure 42]

and, in particular, consideration of how the development of monasteries affected the whole of medieval society.[84]

In the latter part of the twentieth century, science and technology have come to the assistance of the historian and, as Coppack argues, from the 1950s onwards, the study of monastic sites 'passed from those who were primarily motivated by architectural history to those who were primarily archaeologists interested in recording all aspects of the site'.[85] This can be seen by comparing the 1998 plan (Plate 7) with Garton's plan of 1943 (Figure 42) and, in particular, the detail of the guest house in the right-hand corner. The excavations, which yielded this detail, were carried out in the 1960s, but the first record of this new information was in the 1987 guidebook. The site plans did not, however, keep pace with these new archaeological findings.

Today, ecclesiastical archaeology is multi-disciplinary, and, as Greene has pointed out, 'the process is that of "archaeological investigation"', which may or may not involve excavations.[86] This is not to dismiss the findings of the antiquarians and earlier archaeologists, nor to dismiss the interest that the architectural historians took in the ruins, but, as stated above, data can now be obtained on all aspects of monastic history. The claustral area often only represented 10–15% of the site of a religious house, and any site investigation should therefore include all the outer buildings and working areas of the monastery, together with the modifications to and reconstruction of all the main buildings. Modern interpretations of monastic sites should now also consider the history of the site after the Dissolution.

The use of modern sophisticated technological equipment for archaeological surveys has allowed the recording and conservation of monastic sites to advance significantly. An extensive survey of Furness Abbey funded by English Heritage was begun in October 1985 by Jason Wood, the former Assistant Director of the Lancaster University Archaeological Unit. The last plan shown in Plate 3 was published in the latest guidebook produced by English Heritage and co-authored by Wood. As can be seen in Plate 7, the colour coding added by Stuart Harrison, complete with key, serves to make it easier for the general visitor to identify various parts of the site. Figure 44 reproduces the plan of the site contained in the 1993 edition of the 1987 guidebook and is included to allow a comparison of the two latest interpretations of the layout. The dating of the buildings differ in several respects. Plates 1 and 2 illustrate some of the knowledge gained since Hope's and Brakspear's investigations, most of which is as a result of Wood's analysis of the church during the 1980s.[87] This is indicative of the accuracy of modern technological analysis. It

Furness Abbey, record drawing of the chapter house (north exterior) and south transept (south interior). [Figure 43]

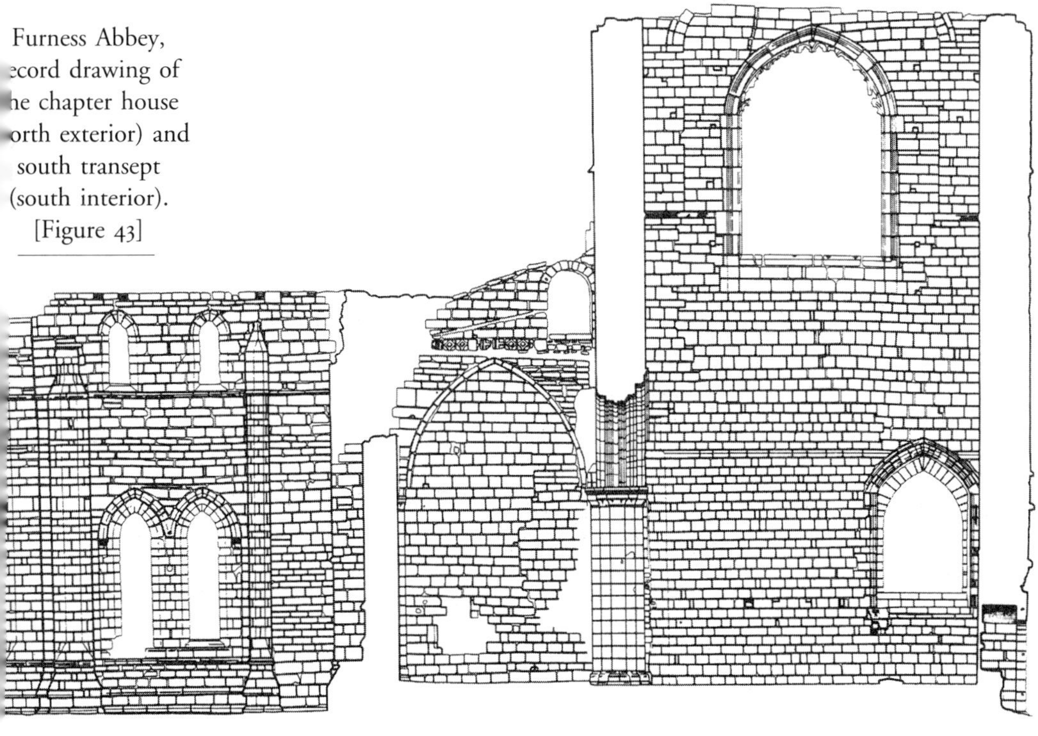

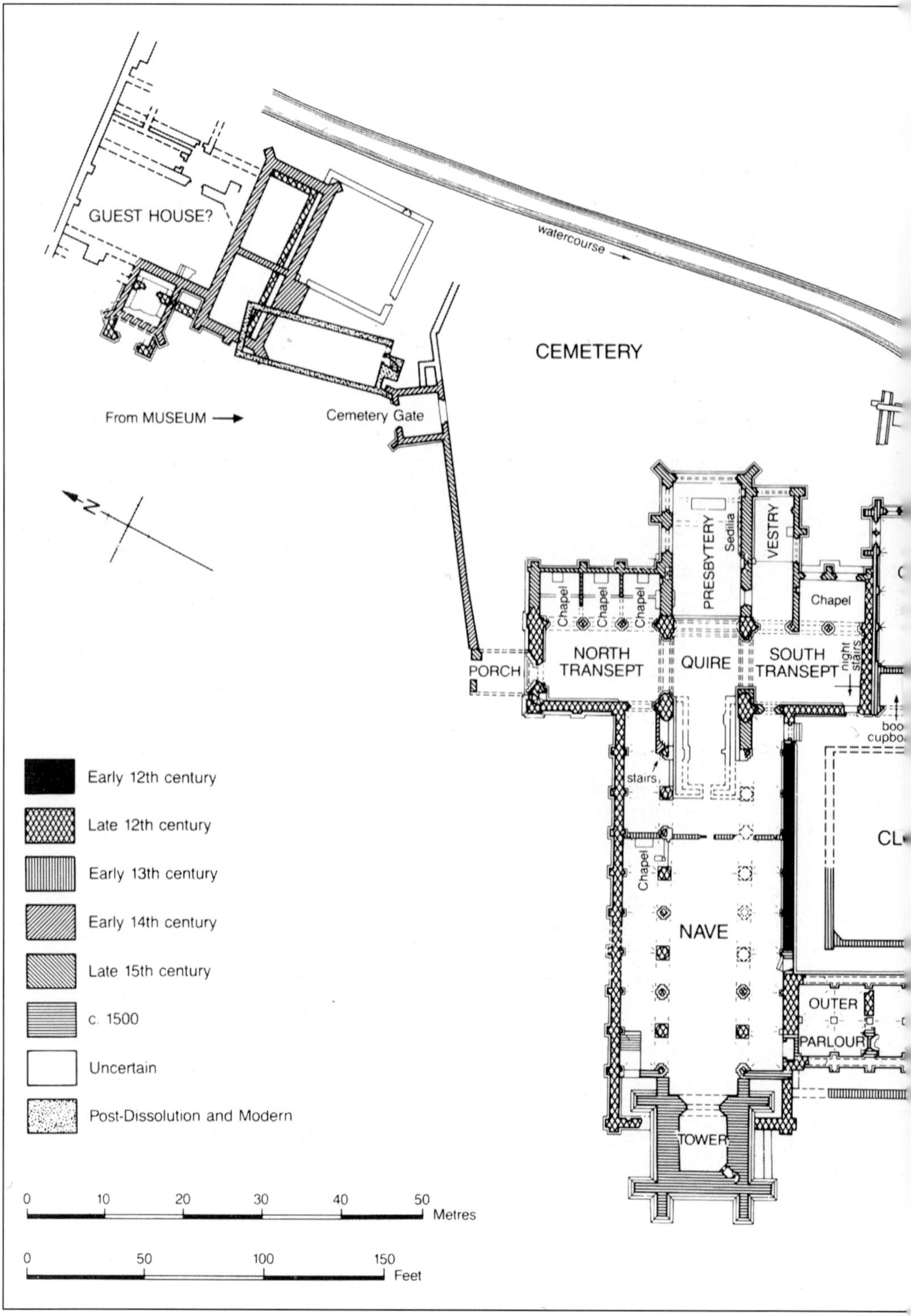
GUEST HOUSE?
watercourse
CEMETERY
From MUSEUM
Cemetery Gate
N
PRESBYTERY
Sedilia
VESTRY
Chapel
Chapel
Chapel
Chapel
NORTH TRANSEPT
QUIRE
SOUTH TRANSEPT
night stairs
PORCH
stairs
Chapel
NAVE
OUTER PARLOUR
TOWER
Early 12th century
Late 12th century
Early 13th century
Early 14th century
Late 15th century
c. 1500
Uncertain
Post-Dissolution and Modern
0 10 20 30 40 50 Metres
0 50 100 150 Feet

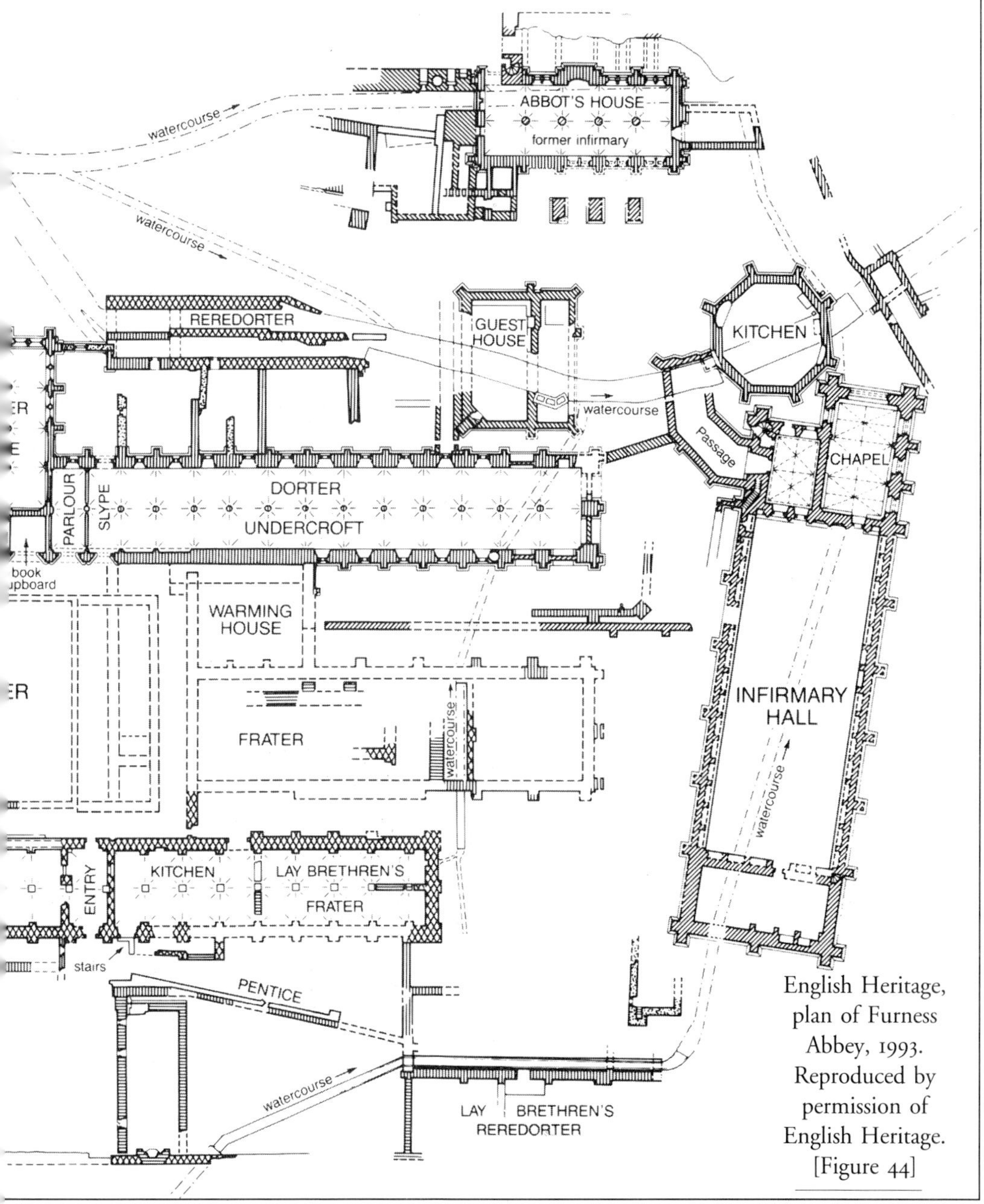

English Heritage, plan of Furness Abbey, 1993. Reproduced by permission of English Heritage. [Figure 44]

also illustrates, as do all the plans over the last two centuries, how interpretation is constantly changing. The 1998 plan may itself be modified in future years.

Wood has compiled detailed stone-by-stone drawings of Furness Abbey based largely on photogrammetry with technical support provided by the Photogrammetic Unit at York University and others. The elevation drawing of Furness Abbey shown in Figure 43, was produced by this method.[88] The drawings which result show the varying types of stone and the types of mortar used, highlight any decayed stonework which requires remedial work, and enable archaeologists to identify the structural phases of the building. Wood argues that 'only survey by means of photogrammetry could provide the volume, homogeneity, accuracy, quality and speed of production of architectural measured drawings'.[89] This technique, combined with detailed analysis of the historic fabric, can therefore provide another interpretation of the abbey and its development. Obviously this method is particularly useful when it is necessary to measure areas which could otherwise not be reached without the aid of scaffolding.[90]

Over 200 stone-by-stone base elevation drawings of Furness Abbey have been prepared by LUAU, but, to date, few of the findings have been published by English Heritage. Jason Wood has written several articles which record the purpose of his work at Furness, together with some of his findings and his views on the future for such methodologies and on what it will mean for furthering our understanding of a monastic site. One obvious observation is that this type of recording and analysis is far less intrusive and destructive than the excavation of trenches.

Wood and his colleagues also produced a computer-aided reconstruction of Furness Abbey using a 3D CAD (Computer Aided Design) programme in collaboration with North Cheshire College. Figure 45 is a computer-generated model of the interior of the nave of the church at Furness.[91] He says of the use of such a computer programme that

> it is not just a display tool, but a research tool. It can show how buildings perform and what it was like to be inside ... we can actually analyse the information, find out why the building fell down and how construction has changed to correct the fault.[92]

In addition to the modern data, the more traditional interpretations of the abbey which have survived in the form of photographs, descriptive accounts, drawings, plans and engravings have also contributed significantly to our understanding of the site. In the same way, whilst Hope's methods were often destructive, especially as a result of the loss of stratigraphical sequences and wholesale clearance of 'rubbish', nevertheless the scholars who have followed in his footsteps have learnt a great deal from his methods.

Furness Abbey, computer generated model of the nave of the church. Reproduced by permission of Jason Wood. [Figure 45]

Wood says in an article written in 1992, which outlined his work at Furness Abbey:

> A thorough search of surviving written and pictorial sources, concentrating on those records dealing with past consolidation and repair works, not only assisted in assessing the extent of earlier fabric interventions but was also particularly valuable in identifying the causes of specific structural failure and building defects. In addition a study of the chief primary and secondary historical sources was commissioned, covering the period from the Savignac foundation through to when the abbey passed into State care in 1923.[93]

Other modern techniques of monastic archaeology have also been developed: the use of field surveys is one example. A knowledge of the post-Dissolution sequence of building is important to our understanding of the medieval structures which may still exist beneath the newer constructions. Field survey can reveal some of this. Geophysical prospecting, which was developed in the 1950s using instruments such as resistivity meters and magnetometers, can help to reveal hidden structures. Aerial photography also helps in placing the ruin firmly in the landscape and can provide evidence of additional buildings located away from the precinct which were, nevertheless, part of the monastic complex. Excavation is still a valid tool for the archaeologist but, by the use of some or all of the above methods, the destructive potential of this technique can be kept to a minimum.

Preservation of the ruins at Furness is still of paramount importance today. Figure 46 is a recent photograph of part of the arch to the chapel house illustrating the friable nature of the red sandstone. The stone crumbles easily, and much of the medieval ornamentation has been lost as a result. More alarming however, is the complete disintegration of keystones in the walls that would, unless replaced, have resulted in the loss of large sections of the walls. Figure 47 is another modern photograph showing how this has, in recent times, been prevented. There has been no attempt to cut and dress the stones to resemble medieval workmanship as previous generations attempted to do. The restoration is simply done to preserve the structure, not reconstruct it.

Since the Bucks' first study, published in 1727, the site and its history have been analysed through many disciplines, and these interpretations have been recorded in text and by visual images. As has been outlined, the methodology of these recordings

Above and this picture: 'Decay and Restoration' photographs of Furness Abbey, 1998. [Figures 46 and 47]

has changed over time. Each one has added further knowledge and has often changed previously conceived ideas. From an initial emphasis on the visual remains, our knowledge expanded as the site was cleared and later explored by archaeologists. More recent non-intrusive techniques have allowed more detailed investigation without risk to the fabric of the building. This more thorough understanding of the building sequence and of the methods of medieval construction has helped in the preservation of the surviving fabric.

At the same time there has also been an awareness that there is no single period of construction; the buildings have evolved over time and the history of the site, and its many buildings, is a continuing process. It can even be argued that the present visitor centre is part of this process.

Research on the site continues today with an independent study being conducted under the guidance of Anne Diss, the Director of Community Action Furness. This study focuses on the outlying buildings in the southern half of the abbey precinct. A monastic garden and a number of projects highlighting the heritage of the surrounding landscape are planned. It is hoped that this will encourage more interest in the site and will complement the work of English Heritage.

Many of the discoveries made by scholars have been related to the public through the medium of guidebooks, and the development of the visitor centre has especially helped to make Furness Abbey a popular tourist attraction. This is the subject of Chapter Four.

Notes

1. D. Lowenthal, *The Past is a Foreign Country* (Cambridge, 1985), pp. xvi–xvii.
2. C. Merewether, 'Traces of loss', in Roth, Lyons and Merewether, *Irresistible Decay*, p. 25.
3. Quote from L. P. Hartley, 'The Go Between', in Lowenthal, *Past is a Foreign Country*, p. xvi.
4. For a short history of the Victoria County Histories, see C. R. J. Currie and C. P. Lewis (eds), *English County Histories: A Guide* (Stroud, 1994).
5. P. Levine, *The Amateur and the Professional* (Cambridge, 1986), p. 20.
6. Ibid., p. 39.
7. J. P. Greene, *Medieval Monasteries* (London, 1995), p. 34.
8. Levine, *Amateur and the Professional*, p. 33.
9. Ibid., p. 39.
10. For an overview of the historical background of antiquarianism and buildings archaeology, see R. Morris, 'Buildings archaeology', in J. Wood (ed.), *Buildings Archaeology: Applications in Practice* (Oxford, 1994).
11. C. Wilson, 'The Cistercians as "Missionaries of Gothic" in Northern England', in C. Norton and D. Park (eds), *Cistercian Art and Architecture in the British Isles* (Cambridge, 1986), p. 86.
12. F. Barnes, *Barrow and District: An Illustrated History* (Barrow, 1951).

13. W. Rodwell, *English Heritage Book of Church Archaeology* (London, 1989), p. 25.
14. G. Coppack, *English Heritage Book of Abbeys and Priories* (London, 1990), p. 22.
15. I. Hunt (ed.), *Norman Nicholson's Lakeland: A Prose Anthology* (London, 1991), p. 192.
16. T. West, *The Antiquities of Furness* (London, 1774), p. 1; see also Currie and Lewis, *English County Histories*, p. 218, for further details regarding West and his work of 1774.
17. West, *Antiquities of Furness* (1774), Preface.
18. The eighteenth-century meaning of the word 'pompous' was probably nearer to our modern word 'magnificent'.
19. West, *Antiquities of Furness* (1774).
20. Ibid., 'Dedication'.
21. Ibid.
22. West, *The Antiquities of Furness* (Ulverston, 1805).
23. West, *Antiquities of Furness* (1813), p. 365.
24. West, *Antiquities of Furness* (1805), p. 75.
25. Beck, *Annales Furnesienses.*
26. J. Walton, *Dalton-in-Furness: A Concise History* (Dalton, 1972), p. 67.
27. Beck, *Annales Furnesienses*, p. 370.
28. Ibid., p. 394.
29. Ibid., p. 397.
30. Ibid., p. 371.
31. Ibid., p. 398.
32. West, *Antiquities of Furness* (1774), p. 94; and Beck, *Annales Furnesienses*, p. 369.
33. Beck, *Annales Furnesienses*, facing p. 390.
34. Ibid., p. 389.
35. Ibid., p. 390. The plate is drawn by H. Shaw and engraved by John Le Keux, Snr.
36. Ibid., p. 368.
37. Ibid., facing p. 390.
38. Ibid., opposite p. 394; and W. H. St John Hope, 'The Abbey of St Mary in Furness', *Trans. of the Cumberland and Westmorland Antiquarian and Archaeological Soc.*, xvi (1900), p. 283.
39. Richardson, *Furness, Past and Present*, ii, pp. 127/8.
40. Beck, *Annales Furnesienses*, double plate, between pp. 378 and 379.
41. Ibid., opposite p. 384.
42. Ibid., p. 381.
43. Ibid., p. 390; West, *Antiquities of Furness* (1774), p. 94. West says of the chapter house roof: 'but its roof hath of late been suffered [proh dolor!] to fall in'.
44. Beck, *Annales Furnesienses*, p. 369.
45. Ibid., p. 373.
46. Ibid., p. 369.
47. Ibid., p. 374.
48. Ibid., p. 383.
49. Ibid., p. 400.
50. Ibid., p. 402.

51. Ibid., p. 403.
52. Barrow Record Office: lc 290B.
53. J. Price, *Sharpe, Paley and Austin: A Lancaster Architectural Practice, 1836–1942* (Lancaster, 1998). See also Edmund Sharpe's own writings which are listed in a monograph which was written to complement an exhibition held at Lancaster University in 1977 to commemorate the centenary of Sharpe's death: R. Jolley, *Edmund Sharpe, 1809–1877: A Lancaster Architect* (Lancaster, 1977).
54. Richardson, *Furness, Past and Present*, ii, facing p. 124.
55. Ibid., i, Preface, p. i.
56. Ibid., ii, p. 141.
57. Ibid., ii, p. 132.
58. Beck, *Annales Furnesienses*, pp. 376, 382; Hope, *Abbey of St Mary in Furness*, pp. 286–7.
59. This plan was not, for reasons unknown, drawn in the usual way, that is by placing the church on an east to west axis.
60. Hope, 'Abbey of St Mary in Furness'.
61. Coppack, *English Heritage Book of Abbeys and Priories*, p. 22.
62. Hope, *Abbey of St Mary in Furness.*
63. Ibid., p. 5.
64. Hope, 'Abbey of St Mary in Furness', p. 225.
65. S. S. Lord, *Delegates' Guide to Barrow-in-Furness and to the Lake and Sea Trips in the District* (Barrow-in-Furness, 1902), p. 6.
66. Hope, 'Abbey of St Mary in Furness', pp. 225–6.
67. Ibid., p. 244.
68. P. Fergusson, *Architecture of Solitude: Cistercian Abbeys in Twelfth-Century England* (New Jersey, 1984), p. 56.
69. Ibid.
70. Coppack, *English Heritage Book of Abbeys and Priories*, p. 24.
71. H. Brakspear, 'On the first church at Furness', *Trans. of the Lancashire and Cheshire Antiquarian Soc.*, xvii (1900).
72. Ibid., pp. 80–6.
73. Richardson, *Furness, Past and Present*, ii, p. 111.
74. P. V. Kelly, 'Dalton Castle', *Trans. Cumberland and Westmorland Antiquarian and Archaeological Soc.*, new ser., xxix (1929), p. 236. This paper was read at Furness Abbey on 19 September 1928. A description of the process of decay can be found in P. E. Hardy, *A Guide to the Care and Preservation of Medieval Cathedrals and Churches* (Essex, 1983), pp. 53–74.
75. J. Ruskin, *The Seven Lamps of Architecture* (London, 1901), p. 358. Further detail on Ruskin's views on the conservation of monuments and on the subsequent establishment of the Society for Protection of Ancient Buildings in 1877 can be found in Chitty, 'Prospect of ruins'.
76. Thompson, *Ruins*, p. 29.
77. H. Emmerson, *The Ministry of Works* (London, 1956), p. 88.
78. Rodwell, *English Heritage Book of Church Archaeology*, p. 26.
79. J. C. Dickinson, 'Furness Abbey: an archaeological reconsideration', *Trans. of the Cumberland and Westmorland Antiquarian and Archaeological Soc.*, new ser., lxvii (1967), p. 54.

80. J. Wood, 'Furness Abbey: an integrated and multi-disciplinary approach to the survey, recording, analysis and interpretation of a monastic building', *Religion and Belief*, vi (1992).
81. Dickinson, 'Furness Abbey', pp. 57–8.
82. S. J. Garton, *The Ancient Monuments and Historic Buildings: Furness Abbey* (London, 1943, 1945, 1950, 1957), p. 1.
83. Dickinson, 'Furness Abbey', p. 75.
84. Rodwell, *English Heritage Book of Church Archaeology*, p. 36.
85. Coppack, *English Heritage Book of Abbeys and Priories*, p. 28.
86. Greene, *Medieval Monasteries*, p. 14.
87. Plate 1: J. C. Dickinson/English Heritage, *Furness Abbey, Cumbria* (London, repr. 1993), p. 21; Plate 2: S. Harrison, J. Wood and R. Newman/English Heritage, *Furness Abbey, Cumbria* (London 1998), p. 5.
88. J. Wood, *Buildings Archaeology*, p. 190.
89. Wood, 'Furness Abbey: an integrated and multi-disciplinary approach', p. 164.
90. J. Wood, 'Record making', in *The Building Conservation Directory* (Tisbury, 1996), pp. 12–13.
91. K. Delooze and J. Wood, 'Furness Abbey Survey Project: the application of computer graphics and data visualisation to reconstruction modelling of an historic monument', in K. Lockyear and S. Rahtz (eds), *Computer Applications and Quantitative Methods in Archaeology 1990* (British Archaeological Reports, International Series, No. 565, 1991). For further information on three-dimensional computer modelling, see J. Wood and G. Chapman, 'Three-dimensional computer visualization of historic buildings: with particular reference to reconstruction modelling', in P. Reilly and S. Rahtz (eds), *Archaeology and the Information Age: A Global Perspective* (London and New York, 1992).
92. Quoted from J. Wood, in J. Stokdyk, 'Drawn from the past', *Building*, 30 Aug. 1991, p. 53.
93. Wood, 'Furness Abbey: an integrated and multi-disciplinary approach', p. 165. Several specialist reports have resulted from the surveys carried out at Furness Abbey. All are listed in ibid., pp. 167–8.

CHAPTER FOUR

Tourists and the Heritage Industry

> Ruins hold out an image of a once glorious present, another time, revealing a place of origin no longer as it was. Their presence is a sign of that loss and of the impossibility of overcoming it.
>
> [Charles Merewether] [1]

> Constituted by memory and distance, ruins are proxies for a past that is continually reinvented by the present.
>
> [Claire Lyons] [2]

When the ruins of a monastic complex are viewed, they raise a number of questions, some of which can never be answered. It is unrealistic to imagine that we can completely reconstruct the past. In Charles Merewether's quote above we are reminded that ruins can be intensely nostalgic and can provoke a desire to claim back what they once stood for but that this is not possible. Claire Lyons, for her part, suggests that the image of ruins can generate memories that, through individual interpretation, can recreate 'a' past which 'fits' with the evidence.

The 'truth' is not just the artist's interpretation as depicted in Chapter Two, or the more detached scholarly view that was examined in Chapter Three. It must include the general visitors' experiences of ruins, which are infinitely more varied. This plurality of usage has been recognised and catered for by all the owners of ruins, particularly since the development of mass tourism, and these varying tastes and interests have in turn been influenced by, and reflected in, the tourist literature that has been produced. Whether it is curiosity, a desire to learn more, or just a leisurely day out, the tourist's motives for visiting a ruin are very personal.

The 'visitor experience' was initially the domain of the elite. By the end of the seventeenth century, the 'classical Grand Tour' of Europe, and in particular of Italy, was a common experience for the sons of the governing classes, the aristocracy and the nobility. John Urry claims that 'Travel was expected to play a key role in the cognitive and perceptual education of the English upper class.' [3] By the late eighteenth century the sons of the professional middle classes were also beginning to experience the benefits of high culture gained through travel. However, by the early years of the nineteenth century, when the Continent was effectively closed to English travellers as a result of the Napoleonic Wars, they had learnt to appreciate their native landscape and its artefacts.

As the century progressed, travel became easier as roads were made more passable, and as the development of the railway system opened up the more isolated places to the traveller. By the end of the nineteenth century the emerging middle classes, who possessed both money and leisure time, were now able to enjoy 'The Tour', albeit in Britain. However, the nature of the traveller's experience was now less adventurous and a certain measure of comfort was sought, not just in the mode of travel, but in the accommodation offered at the end of the journey. The growth of contemporary travel guides reflects this development and the increasing diversity of motives for travelling.

During the twentieth century the rise of mass tourism further opened up the travel market to all classes, and the varying interests of each visitor had to be accommodated. In tandem with the tourist industry, the heritage industry has also grown in importance in recent years and has become more business-orientated as it competed for leisure spending. Heritage can be defined as 'That which a past generation has preserved and handed on to the present and which a significant group of the population wishes to hand on to the future.'[4] This concern for future generations has led to State involvement in the heritage industry and the National Heritage Act of 1983 created the Historic Buildings and Monuments Commission for England, better known as English Heritage. This quasi non-governmental organisation was charged with responsibility for preserving and displaying upwards of four hundred historic buildings or monuments. The philosophy of English Heritage, that of protection and education, is indicative of the way that historical and archaeological sites are interpreted today.

Using images and literature produced since the early decades of the nineteenth century, this chapter will now examine how popular interest in monastic sites, using Furness Abbey as an example, has been developed, fostered, and even exploited, up to the present day.

General travel literature extolling the virtues of the Lake District proliferated during the eighteenth and nineteenth centuries. These publications were aimed at the wealthy visitors to the area. The improvement of roads and coach services encouraged travel amongst the educated elite who had a desire to learn about the area. The literature they were provided with often contained historical and educational material, but these publications were also of a highly personal nature in that, in the tradition of the earlier travellers such as Celia Fiennes and Daniel Defoe, they recounted the experiences and thoughts of the writer.

For example, an early traveller, Edward Baines, published in 1829, an account of his travels that he called a 'family tour'. This popular publication ran to three editions, the second in 1830 and the third in 1834. His book was entitled *A Companion to the Lakes of Cumberland, Westmorland and Lancashire in a descriptive account of a Family Tour and excursion on horseback and on foot.*[5] This work included an account of a visit to Furness Abbey. Baines says that 'a man whom I found digging for stone in the hill-side, became my cicerone, and took me round first to the southern extremity of the Abbey'.[6] He also quotes from Thomas West's scholarly work, *Antiquities of Furness*, and he may also have been aware of West's own travel guide, *A Guide to the Lakes in Cumberland, Westmorland and Lancashire*, which was first printed in 1778 and ran to several editions, the last one being 1821. Baines's work was interspersed with information about the area that might have been of use to other travellers. However, it also included a large number of personal comments and some of his observations were related in a very informal style. For example he says 'As I was leaving the Abbey, a party of two ladies and a gentleman arrived for the purpose of sketching, and they could not have had a finer day for the purpose.'[7]

The disruptions of the French Revolution, the Napoleonic Wars and the Industrial Revolution forced many changes on society. This created a nostalgia for the past which, in comparison, seemed more secure and stable. This interest in a lost world, coupled with the expansion of education and leisure for the middle classes, created inquisitiveness in respect of the tangible remains of past societies. As a result, as Walton and McGloin maintain, 'the market for holidays spread rapidly down the social scale from the mid-Victorian years'.[8]

At the beginning of the Victorian era the expansion of the railways enabled larger numbers of visitors to discover the Lake District, and the creation of the Furness railway line allowed easy access to Furness Abbey. Interest in the excavations at the abbey, which Beck described in his work, also coincided with the building of the railway. Although the abbey was still in private ownership, the increase in public interest in the site was inevitably exploited by the tourist industry for economic gain.

The Furness Railway Company constructed their line primarily to transport the mineral wealth of the region to the coast. It was officially opened on 3 June 1846 and was largely responsible for converting the small port of Barrow, by the early 1880s, from a hamlet of approximately thirty cottages to a large town with a population of 47,000.[9] Passenger traffic was encouraged from the beginning, and a branch line to Rampside established connection with the steamer service to Fleetwood. The Furness Abbey station was opened in 1847 and the railway company leased the land for a nominal rent of £1 per year from the estates of the Earl of Burlington.[10]

Not everyone was enamoured of the railway, however, and John Ruskin, in a lecture given in Oxford in 1884, said about railways in general, and Furness Abbey in particular, that:

> It is continually alleged in Parliament by the railroad, or building companies, that they propose to render beautiful places more accessible or habitable and that their 'works' will be, if anything decorative rather than destructive to the better civilised scene ... Let me take, for instance, for the most beautiful and picturesque subjects once existing in Europe ... Furness Abbey ... A railroad station has been set up within a hundred yards of the abbey.[11]

In a letter dated August 1875, Ruskin wrote of his fears that his 'own sweet Furness abbey would be shaken down by the vibrations from the nearby railway'.[12]

When the railway line was constructed, the abbey site was still part of the Cavendish estates. The manor house, originally built in the abbey grounds by the Preston family in the seventeenth century, was now disused and the Cavendish family sold it to the railway company in 1847 with the express intention that it be used to stimulate the tourist traffic. However, the Cavendish family retained the land upon which it stood and the site of the abbey.

The Manor Ho
Furness Abbe
1727. Reproduc
by permission
the Society o
Antiquaries o
London. [Figure

Figure 48 is a copy of a rare print of the manor house drawn at the instigation of the Society of Antiquaries in 1727.[13] This building, at that time used as a farmhouse, was dilapidated when it came into the possession of the railway company and, over the next two decades, it was largely rebuilt and converted into a hotel. The railway company owned and managed this hotel until they amalgamated with the London, Midland and Scottish Railway in 1923. The hotel was closed in 1938, and, during the Second World War, the hotel, shown in Figure 49,[14] was requisitioned by the army to serve as a gun control centre for Barrow. A German air raid in 1941 badly damaged the building and it was almost completely demolished in 1953. The hotel site is now the car park for the abbey, and the only part of the hotel to survive is the small public bar and restaurant, 'The Abbey Tavern', which was once the station's refreshment room.[15]

The passenger facilities provided by Furness Railway were to prove lucrative both to the general tourist industry of the Lake District and, in particular, to the railway company itself. The railway literally put Furness Abbey on the map and was firmly linked to the abbey's rise as a tourist attraction. In 1853 the number of passengers carried by the company amounted to 95,701 and this had risen only four years later to 188,200.[16] In that same year the Ulverston and Lancaster Railway began to operate a line that connected with the Furness railway and this provided even easier access to the abbey. The grounds of Furness Abbey were chosen to hold a dinner for 300 guests to celebrate the opening of this

-urness Abbey
-tel. Reproduced
- permission of
The Sankey
Collection.
[Figure 49]

line on 26 August 1857. Details of the guest list, which included all the dignities of the area, and a record of the speeches, can be found in Richardson's work.[17] An engraving, shown in Figure 52, illustrates the event and the proximity of the new hotel to the abbey; the marquees that were erected specifically for the inaugural fête can clearly be seen.[18] This was a contemporary drawing reproduced in the *London Illustrated News* of 1857.

The abbey station, completed in 1865, ultimately fared no better than the hotel and the up-platform waiting shelter was destroyed by the same enemy action in May 1941. Figure 51 is a photograph of the station buildings at Furness Abbey,[19] whilst Figure 53 shows the station incorporated in Mackereth's *Seventh Annual Furness Year Book* of 1900 as part of an advertisement for the railway. In the same publication another advertisement for the railway urged that 'Visitors to the lakes should not fail to see the far-famed ruins of St Mary's Abbey.'[20]

By the beginning of the twentieth century, prompted by the General Manager, Mr Alfred Aslett, the Furness Railway was providing a variety of cheap tickets aimed at the tourist market in order to promote the passenger side of their business. This included a widely advertised and successful circular 'Six Lakes' tour, together with an excursion to Furness Abbey. These circular tours were by rail, steam yacht and coach and were heavily advertised.

Passenger services were abandoned on 25 September 1950. The down-

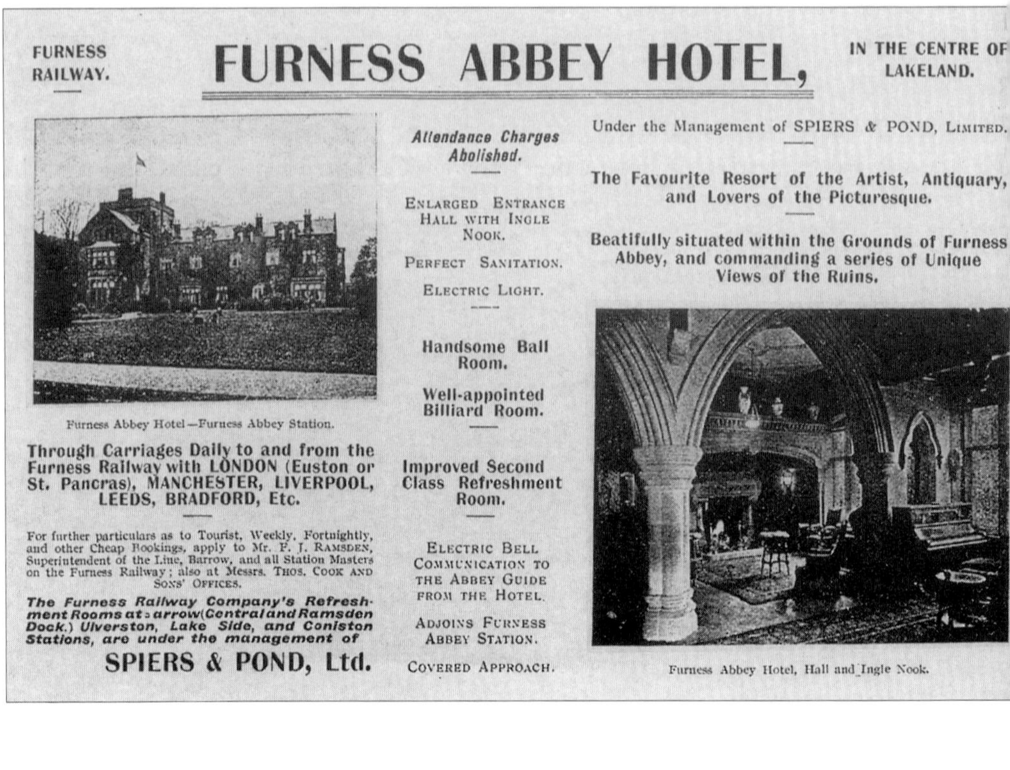

Furness Abbey Hotel, advertisement, 19… [Figure 50]

Furness Abbey Station. Reproduced by permission of The Sankey Collection. [Figure 51]

platform building and signal box were finally dismantled in 1952 and the railway line now runs straight past the abbey.[21]

The cultivation of the abbey as a tourist attraction can be discerned by looking at some of the tourist literature of the time. Figure 54 shows an advertisement from 1916 promoting the railway as a 'Gateway to Lakeland', and the Abbey Hotel is prominently displayed.[22] The abbey ruins, however, seem to be given less prominence than the hotel. The hotel overlooks the ruins, but it is the hotel which is promoted, the ruins are almost an 'added extra'. Figure 50 shows a 1907 advertisement for the hotel and, although it again highlights the close proximity of the abbey ruins and their attraction for the visitor, it is the Lake District which is called 'The favourite Resort of the Artist, Antiquary and Lovers of the Picturesque'.[23]

The advertisement for the hotel, shown in Figure 56, was found in J. P. Morris's *A Handy Guide to the Ruins of Furness Abbey* which was first published *c.*1855.[24] This advertisement can be found in the back of a much later revised edition of Morris's guide, unfortunately undated. However, it must have been after 1923 as it is shown as an LMS hotel, which it became when the London, Midland and Scottish Railway merged with the Furness Railway Company in that year.

'Dejeuner in Furness Abbey, celebration of t[…] opening of the Ulverstone an[…] Lancaster Railwa[…] 1857. [Figure 52[…]

The hotel produced its own glossy tariff book, the front of one edition of which is shown in Figure 57.[25] Unfortunately this too is undated but, as stated on pages 15 and 27 of the brochure, it is still under the management of Messrs Spiers and Pond Limited, and therefore it must have been published before 1913 when the London catering firm ceased to do business with the Furness Railway Company. It is a substantial brochure of approximately forty pages, and the leisure activities available to those staying at the hotel feature prominently. Several little drawings, two of which are shown in Figure 58, serve to illustrate the pleasures of motoring and golfing. The hotel boasts a 'well appointed garage' which stores cars for 1s. 6d. per day and provides a washing facility for an extra charge.[26] This is indicative of the advent of the motor car, used for touring and leisure purposes by the wealthier visitors. Special terms are also offered for visitors' servants at seven shillings per day; this indicates the nature of the hotel's clientele at the time.[27] 'Special Golfing terms' are also set out in the hotel's tariff and fishing trips are advertised, together with other leisure activities such as tennis and croquet on the hotel lawn.[28] The abbey is also advertised in the brochure as a visitor attraction. Ten pages are reserved for a short history and guide to the abbey ruins, but the emphasis is on the status that the abbey gives to the hotel, not the other way around:

The proximity of ruins like those of Furness Abbey – over 700 years

Furness Railway
vertisement, 1900.
[Figure 53]

old, and in point of size the second in the country – would confer prestige on a far less attractive Hotel than the one under consideration.[29]

The Furness Railway Company further exploited the abbey when it copied the Great Seal of Furness Abbey for its coat of arms (see Figure 55).[30] The motto 'Cavendo Tutus' beneath the railway company name means 'Secure by Caution', and this was also the motto of the Cavendish family who were early sponsors of the railway and, of course, the owners of the abbey site.

Whilst the passenger traffic of the railway was increasing, and the abbey hotel was being promoted as providing good accommodation for the tourist of the Lake District, the abbey itself was not being neglected in the tourist literature. This can be seen in the guidebooks that were produced between 1843 and 1998. Several of these will now be assessed in order to explore the various ways that the abbey was being advertised as a tourist attraction to the casual visitor.

By the mid-nineteenth century, there was a market for a guidebook purely devoted to the abbey, for use by those individuals with a more serious interest in the ruins. Although the scholarly works of West and Beck had provided information for the intellectual to study at home, a smaller guide to carry and consult at the site itself was now needed. As transport made the Furness area more accessible, the visitors to the ruins now included a wider public. They came mainly from the middle classes, and they were curious to know more about the ruins, but did not want too much detail. An adequate portable guide to the ruins was not supplied until the 1840s.

The first publication of any importance appears to have been Charles

Furness Railway advertisement, 1916. [Figure 54]

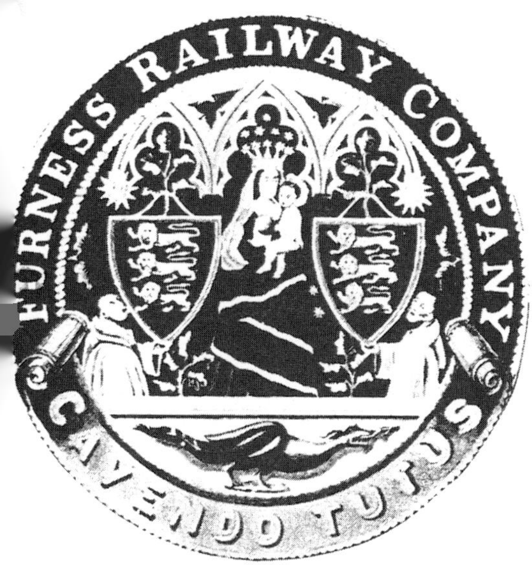

'urness Railway ompany, coat of rms. [Figure 55]

Jopling's *A Sketch of Furness and Cartmel*, printed in Ulverston in 1843. Jopling stated in his preface that he had been asked to supply a much-needed description of Furness Abbey which the general visitor would find useful. His intention was not to bombard the visitor with details since writers such as West had adequately supplied these in larger works.[31] Jopling's work is, nevertheless, quite substantial. It also includes a full description of Furness and Cartmel, their scenery, weather, towns and villages, geology and natural history. The whole work is 273 pages in length, although it is a small book, measuring just 6.5in. × 4in. A ground plan is included on page 110 which is essentially a copy of Close's 1805 plan with a few additions resulting from the clearances. This work continued the traditions of the early tour guides of the Lake District, although it focused primarily on Furness Abbey. This guide was written for the educated and informed reader, and the historical and architectural details of the work were borrowed from the more substantial scholarly works of writers such as West.

Of a similar size, but containing only seventy-seven pages and therefore slightly more accessible, was a *Handbook to the Abbey of St Mary of Furness*, published by Stephen Soulby of Ulverston two years later, in 1845. It is called a 'handbook' and that was exactly what it was. The author, who is unknown, claims that his information is largely derived from Beck's *Annales Furnesienses*, published one year earlier. This makes it a smaller and more manageable version of Beck's scholarly and larger work, and it is therefore a popular version of a book which was originally aimed at the few and which was now available as a guidebook to a wider readership. The ground plan included in the text is a copy of Beck's with an explanation attached.[32] The preface advises the reader that 'The first chapter may be glanced over during the approach to the Abbey, the second may be usefully consulted in the survey of the ruins.'[33] There is, however, no attempt to moderate the language or terminology and the reader is assumed to be well educated, with a superficial, but nevertheless intelligent and informed, interest in the history and architecture of the abbey.

Furness was now firmly established as part of the tourist's, albeit the educated tourist's, itinerary of the Lake District. Guidebooks of the area were published in great quantities from now on, and Furness Abbey features in most of these. Furness Abbey was also well served by its own guides produced specifically for the visitor to the ruins.

A small paperback of thirty-six pages, measuring 3in. × 5.5in., and with a ground plan of the ruins, was produced by W. Porter, a Blackpool publisher, in 1847; it was entitled *A Guide from Blackpool and Fleetwood to Furness Abbey*. This guide was aimed at tourists who were now beginning to find Blackpool an attraction, but who may have wished to travel further afield, perhaps on a day trip. The new railway construction was described in the first few pages, and the route from Blackpool to Poulton by train was outlined. The guide states that:

> The opening of the branch line ... has removed the greatest hindrance to tourists in this direction, and the communication twice daily between Fleetwood and Piel, by an excellent steamer, every way qualified for the task, with the opening of Piel Pier and the Furness Line, has made the chain complete.[34]

The ground plan included on page 22 of this guide, together with a sketchy description of the architecture of the ruins, were taken from Close's edition of West's work of 1805. The hotel is also described and recommended for 'those who may wish to make a lengthened stay at this salubrious and secluded Hotel'.[35] The back of this pocket book includes several advertisements for other hotels in the Fleetwood and Ulverston areas, a good indication of the economic motives for the publication of such a work.

A similar guidebook of twenty-four pages and measuring 3.5in. × 6.5in. entitled *A Guide through the Ruins of Furness Abbey with a Brief Account of Dalton and Pile Fouldry*, was sold for sixpence in 1854. The publication included a brief history of the abbey and a number of engravings of the abbey together with one of the abbey seal. It included a ground plan that is identical to that in the guidebook of 1847.[36]

Another guidebook, published by J. Jackson of Ulverston *c.* 1860 consisted of twenty-four pages and measured 4.5in. × 7in. This was, as with the earlier guides, an appropriate size to put in a pocket. It was entitled *A Handbook to Furness Abbey*. It included a description of the approach by rail to Furness Abbey from Carnforth, addressed itself to 'the numerous admirers of architectural antiquities', and described itself as 'a companion to the far-famed ruins of Furness Abbey'.[37] It also admitted to being 'a brief and bare outline of the history of this once great and magnificent abbey'.[38] The history of the abbey and the description of the ruins were taken from West's *Antiquities of Furness*, although the ground plan has a note appended to it saying that the excavations and discoveries of 1859 have been added to the plan.[39] A romantic poem of eight lines was included at the beginning of the section on the abbey, but no author was credited. This was indicative of the Romantic movement which was

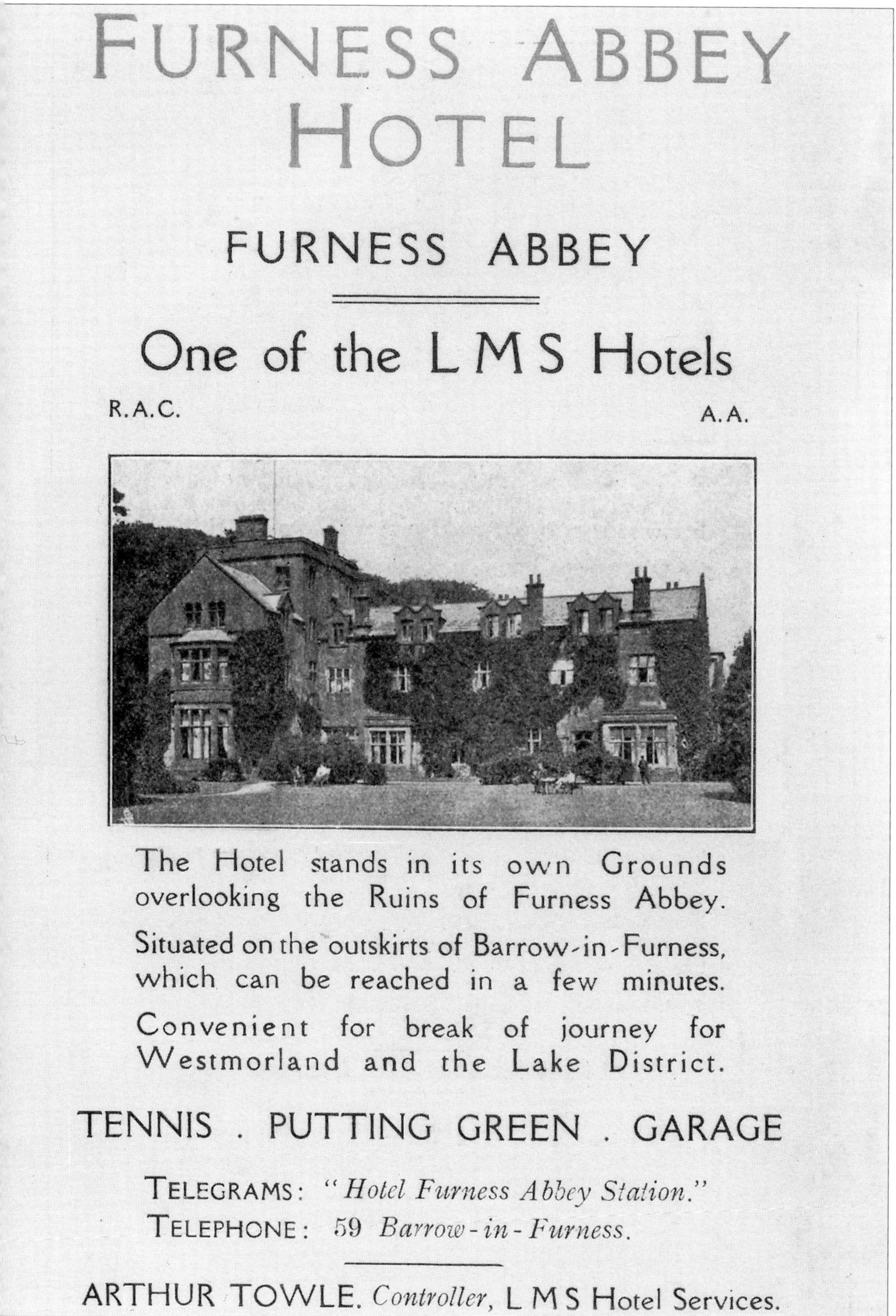

Furness Abbey Hotel, advertisement, after 1923. [Figure 56]

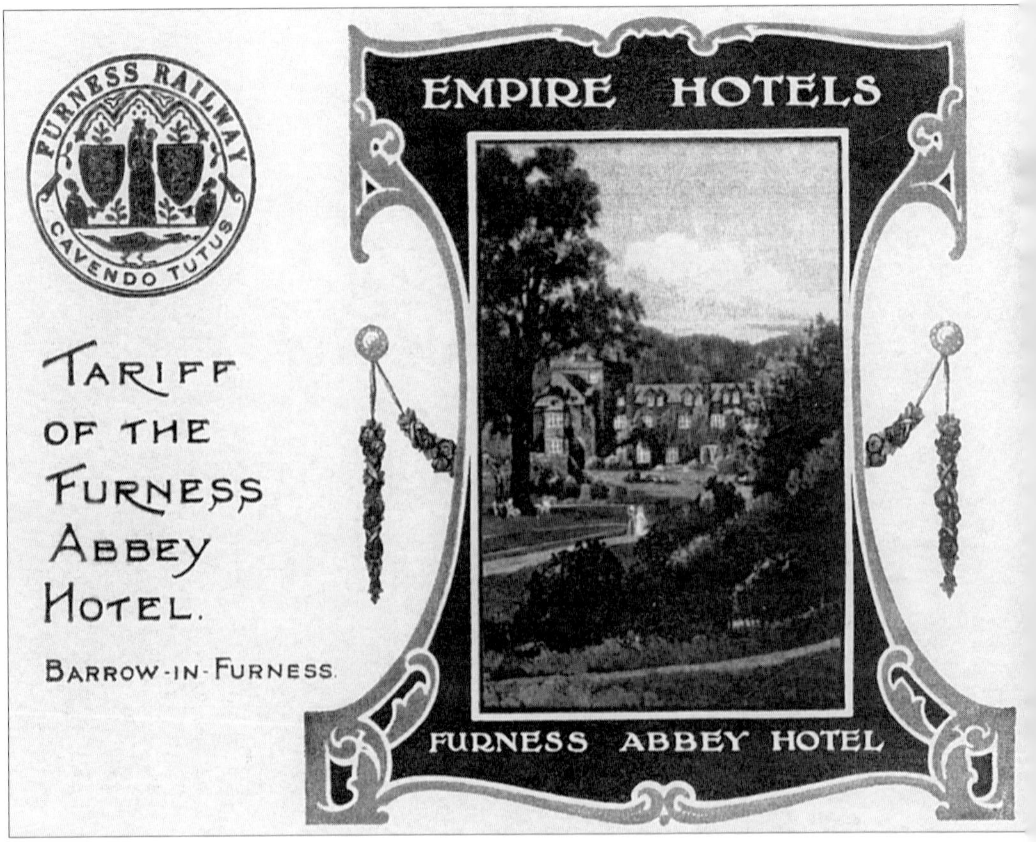

Furness Abbey Hotel Tariff. [Figure 57]

still popular at the time, and which gave the guide a wider appeal than that of the scholarly work of West.

By the middle of the nineteenth century there were a great many guidebooks written with the intention of helping the educated traveller to understand the area he was exploring, and they often included information to aid in the planning of his journey. An early example of a work of this kind for the Lake District is Harriet Martineau's *A Complete Guide to the English Lakes*, originally published in 1855. The 1858 edition of Martineau's travel manual included topographical descriptions, discourses on the meteorology, botany and geology of the region, several woodcuts and a number of engravings. Information on the modes of transport that could be chosen and an indication of the charges for hiring a local driver were also included. Martineau says that 'The drivers are a rather superior sort of men in their vocation, – familiar with the localities, and able to point out all objects of interest to the strangers.'[40] Several tours, excursions and walks are described and one tour includes a visit to Furness Abbey. Although Martineau gives a very brief historical introduction to the abbey, the description of the site is cursory. The tour included an overnight stay

Leisure activities in the Lakes. [Figure 58]

at the nearby Furness Abbey Hotel, 'a handsome and excellent inn' she claimed.[41]

These examples show elements of scholarly borrowing and aspire to a certain accuracy in their descriptions. Most include a plan of the grounds, now considered vital for an understanding of the ruins. The guide published by Jackson *c.*1860 also contained updated information reflecting new archaeological discoveries. All the guides demonstrate an awareness that Furness Abbey was a tourist attraction in its own right, but also recognise that there were other interesting places to visit in the area, some of which are described. The language is aimed at educated visitors, who now included the heterogeneous middle classes, and the contents suggest that the authors all had similar interests. Presumably these guides were sold in the local towns and possibly at the railway stations and steamship terminals, and there can be no doubt that they were produced for commercial reasons.

The economic 'exploitation' of the visitor is very evident in a popular guidebook by H. Barber, originally published as *Shaw's Tourists' Picturesque Guide to Furness Abbey*. The eighth edition, published *c.*1878, was sold at a price of one shilling.[42] Of the hundred pages included in this publication, which measures 4in. × 6.5in., twenty-five are advertisements. The fact that the book was inscribed to His Grace the Duke of Devonshire, owner of Furness Abbey at the time, who was Chairman of the Board of Directors of the Furness Railway, also indicates the interest of the railway company in its publication. This is reinforced on the first page where the benefits of travelling by railway are extolled. The approach, by rail, to Furness Abbey is described and a brief history of each station is included. The Furness Abbey guide was one of a series of guidebooks produced by Norton and Shaw who were apparently noted for their personally conducted tours, especially in the 'romantic' tourist districts of Northern Ireland. Several advertisements for their services indicate that the nature of their business was that of railway and steamboat agents.

The eighth edition of this particular publication had been revised and new plates and a folded map of the district had been included. Three of the twelve tinted plates show views of Furness Abbey,[43] and there is a ground plan displayed between pages 34 and 35. The new plates are accompanied by an expression of hope that they would add to the tourists' pleasure and provide a 'really "picturesque" guide'.[44]

The architectural description of Furness Abbey is couched in very romantic and picturesque language, and a few lines of poetry are included. There is, however, also a strong scholarly element in the contents which assumes an informed reader. It includes a fairly detailed guide to the architecture of the main buildings of the abbey and laments the abbey's demise in architectural terms. The perpetrators of this destruction, the guide tells us, are responsible for 'plunging the nation into an abyss of barbaric architecture, which produced the "hideous painted and white-washed parallelograms" that have been raised up and called churches in later times'.[45] The plundering of the stones, evidence of which, we are told, can be found in numerous houses in the district, was also condemned by the writer.[46]

It would appear that the 'picturesque' qualities of the ruins were still important to the reader of Shaw's guides but it is interesting to note that the author comments on the vegetation adorning the walls by saying that: 'All these plants add considerably to the picturesqueness and romantic appearance of the ruins, yet ... they slowly, but surely, help on the work of destruction.'[47] The vibration caused by the heavy mineral trains, which were now regularly thundering past the ruins, was also commented upon, and the fact that a 'large portion of the eastern side of the lantern tower [has] lately [fallen] in with a great crash' was noted in the guide.[48] Both concerns show an early recognition of a need to preserve the remaining structures.

The historical sketch which complemented the tour of the grounds was written in a scholarly way and included a translation of the foundation charter and the surrender charter of the abbey. There was also an impression of the abbot's seal with a description. Included at the back of the text was an alphabetical index of the places and names cited in the work.

By 1882, Edwin Waugh, in volume VII of his *Complete Works* declined to provide an architectural description of the ruins because lack of space in his own work prohibited it, but he states that 'the visitor can buy all that information for a trifle on the spot itself'.[49] This seems to indicate that the tourist was able to buy information leaflets at the abbey site, perhaps in the hotel or at the small custodian's hut, which is thought to be of Victorian origin and which can still be found behind the west tower.

In the same year as Waugh's publication, the *History and Directory of Furness and Cartmel*, published by Mannex, was produced. This included a very full account of the abbey, its history and a description of the ruins. It begins: 'the vista of ruins bursts like some fairy enchantment upon the vision' and 'its walls ... are crowned with a rich garland of ivy, which, like Omnipotence enthroned, mocks the majesty of man'.[50] The language is part scholarly and part flowery and is embellished with lines of poetry. An earlier Mannex Directory printed in 1876 explains the motive for the inclusion of a description of the abbey in the publication by claiming that interest in the ruins had never, since the time of the Dissolution, been as keen as it is today (1876).[51]

Local pride in the abbey is reflected in these directories, especially those published at the end of the nineteenth century which coincided with the renewed archaeological interest created by Hope. A publication, by S. S. Lord, which was produced by the Ancient Order of Foresters in 1902 entitled *Delegates' Guide to Barrow-in-Furness and to the Lake and Sea Trips in the District* is written proof, if proof is needed, of the success of Barrow in the nineteenth century, the pride of the inhabitants in their town and their belief in a promising future. This work is highly readable and contains a lot of interesting information about the town and its industries and, in particular, about the local dignitaries who had helped to make it successful. Chapter Seven of the publication is devoted to a history of Furness Abbey, although the abbey is also mentioned on several other occasions throughout the work. The visitor is directed to the abbey from Barrow and great emphasis is placed on Barrow's connection with it. This is reinforced by a comparison that is provided between the industrious nature of the monks, which proved to be the reason for their success, and the industrious nature of the people of Barrow in modern times: 'Their history, in fact, proves how much can be accomplished even by small means and limited resources when once work is tackled by vigour and with a determination to succeed.'[52]

The affluence of industrialised Barrow mirrors the nation-wide situation. The middle-class optimism of the Victorian era carried through into the Edwardian period, although with hindsight we know that this was under threat as Britain's industrial supremacy was being undermined and war was on the horizon. During this period innovations, such as the internal combustion engine and improved production methods, led to the marketing of a widening range of consumer durables including the motor car and the bicycle. This, coupled with increasing leisure opportunities for the middle classes ensured the growth of the tourist industry. This growth continued and, in the decades between the wars with rising living standards extending down the social scale, the expansion of car ownership, the growing interest in the countryside and the concept of paid holidays affecting increasing numbers of workers, mass tourism became a reality. This interest accelerated further between 1955 and 1973 when unemployment was low, living standards were rising and paid holidays were being accepted as normal and necessary. Car ownership was also rising, and by 1972 statistics show that there were sixteen million cars on the roads, thus giving the British traveller more independence.[53]

National awareness of the need to care for and protect the country's heritage, which emerged in the last decades of the nineteenth century, was being actively pursued as interest in tourism grew. One of the consequences of this was the move towards State ownership of ancient monuments. This not only ensured that, as guardians of an ancient site, the State could exercise its duty to preserve the remaining structure, but it also ensured that all such sites were now opened to the public. In its capacity as guardian, the State's duty was to preserve the fabric of the buildings in its care, but not to restore or in any way alter the original form. After initial remedial work had been completed, a site was opened to the public for a small admission charge. A full-time custodian was appointed and all site staff were provided with black uniforms, reminiscent of prison wardens.[54]

The Ministry of Works took guardianship seriously: consumer unfriendly notices admirably reflected this approach. They welcomed visitors to their sites with metal plaques on walls warning that:

> ANY PERSON WRITING ON OR SCRATCHING THE FABRIC
> OF THIS MONUMENT WILL BE LIABLE TO PROSECUTION

It was recognised that visitors arrived at the abbey with their own agendas and, although some would wish only to wander in the grounds without requiring any knowledge of what they were looking at, others would want more information. Official guidebooks were therefore provided at the most important monuments. These guidebooks also appeared to be in uniform, each covered in a dark blue cover. Only the title on the front distinguished one from the other and the style hardly varied. They were written by professionals and were illustrated with a few black and white photographs. They always included a ground plan, which was often folded at the back of the pamphlet. In 1935 the Ministry of Works published a series of illustrated regional guides. The first one listed all the ancient monuments under their care in northern England with a brief history of each. They were intended 'to supplement the more detailed archaeological data available by the more general and popular account of all the monuments in a group of counties'.[55]

Although archaeological excavations at certain sites, Furness Abbey included, were allowed by the Ministry of Works, provided that the results were published, the emphasis was on the administration and safeguarding of the sites, rather than on encouraging research.[56] A study of the guidebooks reveals that the interests of the general public were also considered to be unimportant, in that the guides did not present information in an attractive and consumer friendly style which would be accessible to the lay person. This was despite the fact that the sites were now in public ownership and interest in them had extended to a larger proportion of the population.

Despite the early lack of encouragement, interest in heritage interpretation continued to grow. In 1957 Freeman Tilden in his book *Interpreting Our Heritage* formulated a philosophy of heritage interpretation: 'through interpretation, understanding, through understanding, appreciation, through appreciation, protection'.[57] By 1995 Herbert was arguing that 'The early determinant of wealth and means have largely been replaced by tastes and preferences. Very few places remain the preserve of the wealthier, more educated section of society.'[58]

By 1923 Furness Abbey had passed into State control and was administered by the Ministry of Public Building and Works. Their interpretation of the Furness Abbey ruins was initially limited to the Official Guidebooks published by HMSO. The first such guidebook, referred to in Chapter Three, was written by Garton and published in 1943. The second guidebook published in 1965 and written by Dickinson was, at the time, the standard text for any visitor wishing to understand the structural remains before him.[59] Although several editions were published, the format varied little and included, in approximately twenty-five pages, a summary, a history of the abbey and buildings, a description of the standing buildings and a glossary. The descriptions contained in these pamphlets lacked detail but were accurate for the time and written in a scholarly fashion. The general visitor, however, may have found the contents a trifle dull and uninspiring. All 'romantic language' and the addition of personal observations had now been eradicated and they were very clearly 'functional' guides.

A key was included with the plan to enable the visitor to date the standing structures, but as this was produced in black and white with the use of shading and patterns to delineate the dates, the result could be confusing. The scale was shown in feet and metres to reflect the recent change to metrication. Apart from the addition of minor details and the renaming of several of the buildings, this plan is similar to the 1943 plan shown in Figure 42, also published by HMSO, which may reflect the lack of new evidence since the early excavations. Although, as noted earlier, there were additional excavations on the site in the 1960s, these were not reflected in a published guidebook until 1987.

The 1970 edition of the Furness Abbey guide contains four photographs, but two of them, the chapter house and the church looking towards the transepts and presbytery, have been printed with the negatives round the wrong way, which obviously also reverses the details of the buildings. As so much emphasis is placed on correct alignments in monastic buildings, this is a curious error.[60]

Therefore, despite the onset of mass tourism, the guidebooks of Furness Abbey did not reflect this growing interest. However, by the 1980s, it was acknowledged that the tourist should influence how the site is presented. A new commercial ethic emerged with the inception, in 1983, of English Heritage. This new body was charged with the responsibility of actively promoting the interest, enjoyment and education of the public in respect of the buildings and conservation areas in its care. The name, English Heritage, was chosen to represent the purpose of the organisation, and a simple logo was adopted to catch the public's eye.[61]

Although partly funded by the State, English Heritage was also required to raise funds itself by displaying its monuments as tourist attractions. The passive nature of guardianship previously espoused by the Department of the Environment, the former custodians of the site, had now been abandoned in favour of a more aggressive approach. Emphasis was still placed

Reconstruction of Furness Abbey attributed to R. W. Johnson [Figure 59]

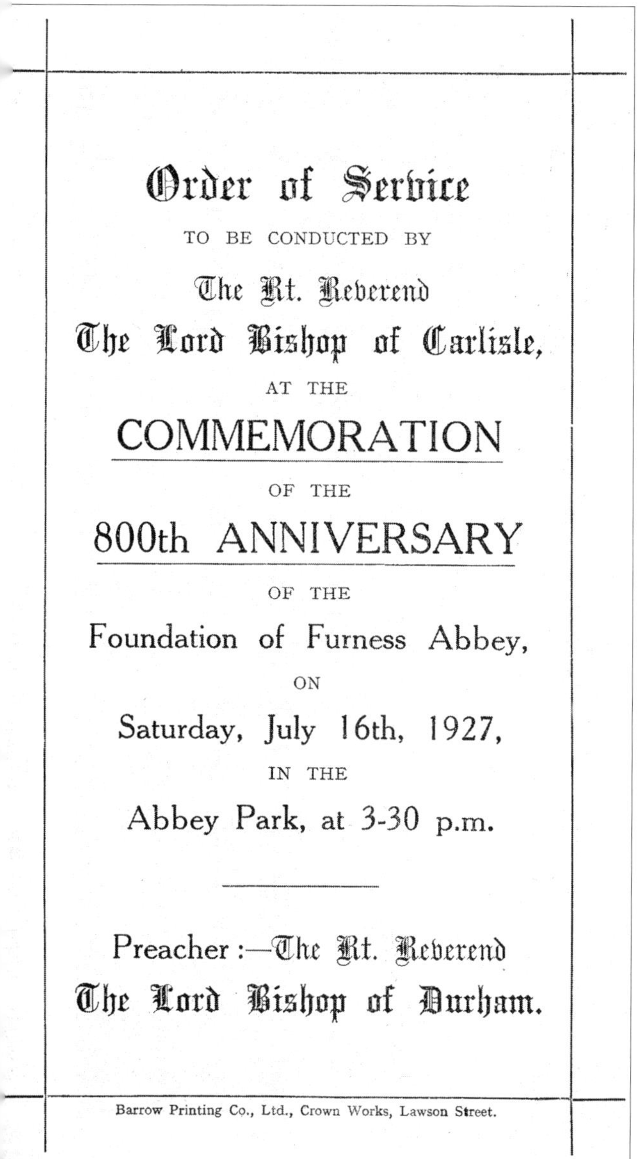

Order of Service

TO BE CONDUCTED BY

The Rt. Reverend

The Lord Bishop of Carlisle,

AT THE

COMMEMORATION

OF THE

800th ANNIVERSARY

OF THE

Foundation of Furness Abbey,

ON

Saturday, July 16th, 1927,

IN THE

Abbey Park, at 3-30 p.m.

Preacher :—The Rt. Reverend

The Lord Bishop of Durham.

Barrow Printing Co., Ltd., Crown Works, Lawson Street.

Order of Commemoration Service, 1927. [Figure 60]

on preservation, but the promotion of heritage sites as tourist attractions had become increasingly important. A fundamental aspect of English Heritage's success, therefore, depended on its ability to increase interest in the places under its guardianship.

To achieve this, new uniforms were introduced, this time with the emphasis on informality, and visitor centres were built to house the artefacts found on site, the tourist literature, the wide range of merchandise and the displays constructed to aid the visitor's understanding of the site. Furness Abbey has benefited from all the above, and the new visitor centre, although small, is attractively laid out and includes a small museum to replace the less than adequate infirmary chapel as a place of storage for the portable fragments found on site.

The educational aspect of heritage is strongly emphasised by English Heritage. At the Furness Abbey visitor centre there is an area devoted to wall charts illustrating the history of the abbey in an easy to read and visually pleasing form. An audio tape, which serves as a guided tour of the grounds, is included in the admission price. This provides a great deal of information about the buildings and their history and yet is convenient to use and unintrusive to other visitors. Children are welcomed, and a 'school' room is provided for the use of large parties. Various drawings and photographs are on display in this room, and a few 'hands on' models and jigsaws are available for the very small child. Occasionally a guide is on hand to take a party around the abbey grounds and on request, a local man, Iain McNichol (known as the History man), dresses up in a white monk's habit and becomes Brother John for school parties. The children are also encouraged to dress up, and a set of smaller robes can be found in the visitor centre for this purpose. A lump of sandstone is provided in the museum for visitors to touch to experience for themselves how friable the abbey buildings are. A visitors' book is also available for those who want to record their own impressions.

A visit to the site provides evidence of the individual and personal experiences of the tourist. The small child wishing to know what the abbey was originally like can visualise this by looking at the large display board outside the visitor centre, which shows a reconstruction of the abbey church (Figure 59).[62] A party of schoolchildren wanting to sit on the stones to eat their sandwiches can do so without hindrance. The visitor wanting to take a memento back home with him can purchase a souvenir from the shop or take a photograph of the buildings. A tourist wanting to soak up the atmosphere, so loved by the nineteenth-century romantics, can wander at leisure amongst the ruins with no time limit, and no one to tell him not to walk on the grass or sit on the walls. A child can fantasise that the book cupboards on either side of the vestibule of the chapter house used to be the dungeons as there are no plaques or notices to tell her otherwise and spoil her imagination. When the newly married couple want to use the abbey ruins as a backdrop for their photographs, they are not prevented. When the budding historian wants to touch the very stones that were once the home of a thriving medieval community, there is no one to deny her that pleasure. Even the modest modern building of the visitor centre is placed away from the ruins, and the toilets, such an important requisite for any isolated site, are out of public view.

The original purpose of the abbey was religious and although little has been said of that in this work, there are people who still think of it as a religious site and there have been moves during the last century to reclaim it as such.

Mass, 1992. Reproduced by permission of Ali Leach. [Figure 6

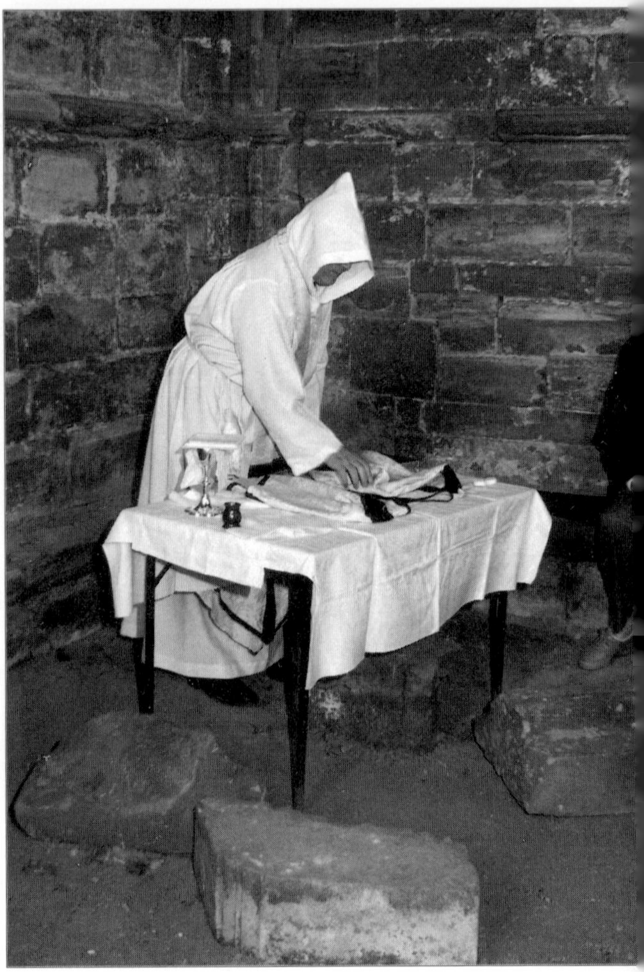

So, the history of the site has come full circle. Figure 60 is the front of the 'Order of Service' pamphlet produced in 1927 to commemorate the 800th anniversary of the foundation of the abbey, and a service was held in the Abbey Park by the Rev. Lord Bishop of Carlisle.[63] In 1990 a mass was held in the infirmary chapel conducted by an eighty-two-year-old monk, the Very Rev. Dom Hugh Menken,[64] and in 1992 Bishop Brewer celebrated mass in the main church for the first time since the Dissolution (see Figure 61).[65]

The diverse interests and the economic potential of the visiting public have therefore been recognised by English Heritage over the last fifteen years. However, this attitude was not adequately reflected in the abbey guidebooks until 1998. Dickinson, the author of the later editions of the Ministry of Works' guidebook, was also responsible for the production of the first guidebook to be issued by English Heritage in 1987. This was simply a reprint of the guide previously published by the Department of Environment in 1983. The 1993 edition, although slightly glossier and formatted in a more modern style, differs little from the guidebooks of the previous four decades. The plan is labelled 'Tour' and, apart from the outline detail of a possible guesthouse in the north-east corner, it is identical to the plan to be found in the 1970 edition of the guidebook. Other minor differences between this guidebook and those produced by the Ministry of Works include the title, which now states that Furness Abbey is in Cumbria, the scale, which has been changed to metric, and the identification of the museum.[66]

However, to complement English Heritage's more modern image, a new guidebook was published in 1998. Although written by archaeologists and historians, it conveys a holistic approach to the abbey ruins. It is very attractively produced with plenty of colour images, and the 'tour' is amply illustrated with colour photographs of the buildings. It includes a new, colour coded, foldout plan which is very easy to follow (shown in Plate 7).[67] This plan incorporates the new knowledge gained through the technological advances of the 1980s, and the new guide also includes a plan of the precinct similar to that produced by Hope and shown in Plate 9. This has been updated to include the modern additions, including the museum and car parks.[68]

The history of the abbey in this latest publication has been extended to include the post-Dissolution period, and there is a section on the 'Picturesque and Romantic' movement as discussed in Chapter Two of this book. The Furness Abbey Hotel and station are recognised for the first time for the part they played in the reclaiming of the ruins. There is also a section on the nearby Piel Castle although this, in contrast with the earlier nineteenth-century guides, is the only reference to other sites of interest in the area.

A wide audience is targeted in this publication, reflecting the varying interests of visitors. Even the scholarly are provided with a list of further publications for future consultation. The language used is not overly technical and the design is accessible to the average tourist.

English Heritage has been charged with the conservation of the abbey, and the Chief Executive's Statement in the Annual Report of 1996/97 focuses on the importance of knowledge in enhancing the visitor experience and also in securing long-term conservation by promoting interest in the monuments in its charge.[69] This emphasis contrasts with the Ministry of Works' passive attitude which stressed the role of guardian but provided little in the way of encouragement to anyone interested in the site for anything other than its monastic past. Today the ruins of Furness Abbey are displayed in an attractive and accessible way and it is left to the visitors themselves to select that which interests them most. The abbey is no longer the preserve of the elite, as described in the first section of this chapter. The modern view is that a specialised knowledge of Furness Abbey is not required to enjoy the ruins; in fact even a basic knowledge of the history of the site is not essential for some visitors. A visit to Furness Abbey may merely provide a pleasant, leisurely day out.

Notes

1. Merewether, 'Traces of loss', in Roth, Lyons and Merewether, *Irresistible Decay*, p. 25.
2. C. Lyons, 'Archives in ruins', in ibid., p. 79.
3. J. Urry, *The Tourist Gaze: Leisure and Travel in Contemporary Societies* (London, 1990), p. 4.
4. Quoted from the 1983 National Heritage Conference, in D. T. Herbert (ed.), *Heritage, Tourism and Society* (London, 1995), p. 8.
5. E. Baines, *A Companion to the Lakes of Cumberland, Westmorland and Lancashire in a descriptive account of a Family Tour and excursion on horseback and on foot* (2nd edn, London, 1830).
6. Ibid., p. 227.
7. Ibid., p. 231.
8. J. K. Walton and P. R. McGloin, 'The tourist trade in Victorian Lakeland', *Northern History*, xvii (1981), p. 153.
9. K. J. Norman, *Railway Heritage: The Furness Railway. A Recollection* (Peterborough, 1994), p. 7.
10. Ibid., p. 23.
11. E. T. Cook and A. Wedderburn (eds), 'The art of England', in *The Works of John Ruskin*, vol. XXXIII (London, 1908), p. 404.
12. J. Ruskin, 'Fors Clavigera', letter 56, Aug. 1875.
13. Dickinson, 'Furness Abbey'.
14. Furness Abbey Hotel, Photo no. 7387, The Sankey Collection.
15. Ibid., p. 24.
16. J. Melville and J. L. Hobbs, 'Early railway history in Furness', *Trans. of the*

Cumberland and Westmorland Antiquarian and Archaeological Soc., tract ser., xiii (1951), p. 45.

17. Richardson, *Furness, Past and Present*, i, p. 21.
18. Lancaster City Museum, LM 98.88.
19. Furness Abbey Railway Station, Photo no. 0133, The Sankey Collection.
20. H. W. Mackereth, *Furness Year Book* (Ulverston, 1900), p. 377.
21. Norman, *Railway Heritage*, p. 22.
22. Ibid., opposite title page.
23. Ibid., p. 23.
24. Morris, *Handy Guide to the Ruins of Furness Abbey.*
25. *Tariff of the Furness Abbey Hotel* (Barrow-in-Furness).
26. Ibid., p. 35.
27. Ibid., p. 29.
28. Ibid., pp. 25, 27.
29. Ibid., p. 5.
30. A. C. Parkinson, *A History of Catholicism in the Furness Peninsula 1127–1997* (Lancaster, 1998), p. 103.
31. C. M. Jopling, *A Sketch of Furness and Cartmel comprising the Hundred of Lonsdale North of the Sands* (Ulverston, 1843).
32. *Handbook to the Abbey of St Mary of Furness*, between pp. 20 and 21.
33. Ibid., Preface.
34. *A Guide from Blackpool and Fleetwood to Furness Abbey, with a ground plan of the ruins* (Blackpool, 1847), p. 7.
35. Ibid., p. 11.
36. *A Guide through the Ruins of Furness Abbey with a Brief Account of Dalton and Pile Fouldry* (Ulverston, 1854).
37. *A Handbook to Furness Abbey: with a Short Account of the Pile of Fouldrey and Rampside to which is appended a condensed description of the Lake District* (Ulverston, *c.* 1860), p. 4.
38. Ibid., p. 7.
39. Ibid., p. 15.
40. H. Martineau, *A Description of the English Lakes* (published as *The English Lakes*, Windermere, 1858; repr. Wakefield, 1974), p. 15.
41. Ibid., p. 17.
42. H. Barber, *Shaw's Tourists' Picturesque Guide to Furness Abbey, The Vicinity and Lakes Coniston and Windermere* (8th edn, London, *c.* 1878).
43. Ibid., pp. 32, 43, 45.
44. Ibid., Preface.
45. Ibid., p. 33.
46. Ibid., p. 47.
47. Ibid., p. 48.
48. Ibid.
49. E. Waugh, *Waugh's Complete Works: Rambles in the Lake Country*, vol. VII (Manchester, 1882), p. 64.
50. *History and Directory of Furness and Cartmel* (publ. Mannex, Preston, 1882), pp. 62–3.

51. *History and Directory of Barrow-in-Furness and the whole of North Lonsdale* (publ. Mannex, Preston, 1876), p. 111.
52. Lord, *Delegates' Guide to Barrow-in-Furness*, p. 11.
53. J. Stevenson, *British Society, 1914–1945* (London, 1984), p. 391. See also p. 390: 'private car ownership reach[ed] 2 million by 1939'; and p. 393: 'In the early 1920s only 1.5 million people had paid holidays, by 1939 [it was] over 11 million'.
54. A. Eastaugh and N. Weiss, 'Broadening the market', in D. L. Uzzell (ed.), *Heritage Interpretation*, vol. II: *The Visitor Experience* (London, 1989), p. 60.
55. Rt. Hon. Lord Harlech, *Ancient Monuments in the care of the Ministry of Works: Illustrated Regional Guide No. 1: Northern England* (1st edn, London, 1935; repr. 1951), p. 5.
56. Emmerson, *Ministry of Works*, p. 86.
57. Quoted in D. Light, 'Heritage as informal education', in Herbert, *Heritage, Tourism and Society*, p. 121.
58. Herbert, *Heritage, Tourism and Society*, p. 216.
59. J. C. Dickinson, *Furness Abbey, Lancashire* (London, 1965).
60. J. C. Dickinson, *Furness Abbey, Lancashire* (London, 1970), pp. 18, 20.
61. Eastaugh and Weiss, 'Broadening the market', p. 60.
62. Barnes, *Barrow and District.*
63. Barrow Public Library: lc 290F1.
64. 'First Abbey Mass said in 450 years', *Evening Mail*, Friday 21 Sep. 1990.
65. Photograph kindly provided by A. Leach.
66. J. C. Dickinson, *Furness Abbey, Cumbria* (London, 1993).
67. Harrison, Wood and Newman/English Heritage, *Furness Abbey, Cumbria*, back page.
68. Ibid.
69. English Heritage, *Annual Report and Accounts*, 1996/97, p. 8.

CHAPTER FIVE

Conclusion

> The call of the past can, of course, be translated in various ways and made to carry many messages. And the convalescence of an artifact – its separation from contemporary life – can be short-lived when pressed into some new use within the context of religion, politics, or aesthetics.
>
> [Michael S. Roth] [1]

After over nine hundred years of Cistercian history all that survives today in England are the ruins of their once great monastic houses. After the Dissolution, these disintegrating structures remained largely hidden from view and abandoned, except as quarries for stone. However, once the initial shock of their destruction had mellowed into complacency, and nature had removed the starkness of their broken and jagged edges, monastic buildings were reclaimed. Their history continued in a form that no monk had ever envisaged.

The history of monastic ruins continues to evolve through the varying interpretations of the people who reclaimed them. The artists and writers, who were the focus of the second chapter, derived inspiration from viewing the site and did not seek to preserve what they saw. Yet what they recorded in writing and pictures does have the effect of arresting the decay by freezing it at a point in time. They identified the ruins with the landscape and as part of nature; their reclaiming of the ruins was of an intensely personal nature.

The scholars, who were the subjects of the third chapter, reclaimed the site in order to understand the past, to learn about what the ruins could reveal about history and architecture. In order to reconstruct that history, they had to uncover the remains, even though in the process they were often responsible for destroying some of the evidence. Yet the knowledge that was gained, and can still be gained from further excavations, has enhanced our understanding of the monastic site and has prompted further investigation through technology and historical discourse.

Once it was understood that the ruins were of a fragile nature and vulnerable to erosion, the need to conserve was of paramount importance. Yet, in order to provide a justification for conservation, and to generate income to support this process, it was necessary to develop a more widespread interest in monastic sites. This pluralistic interest in the form of tourism and the heritage industry was explored in Chapter Four.

This study has demonstrated how the material remains of monastic communities continue to fascinate. This may be manifested in a desire to reconstruct a bygone age that in some way helps us to understand the present, or in a desire to escape from the complexities of modern living and to conjure up the perceived innocence of the past. However, a ruin can also be valued for what it is rather than what it used to be. It can be appreciated as an art form or as a spiritual or romantic place and can be enjoyed in the same way as any landscape.

It has been argued that all these interpretations of monastic ruins are equally valid for historians. The pictorial and written evidence that they have produced has become part of the history of the site – a history that will continue to evolve as long as some of the original structure remains visible. Moreover, a study of the various interpretations of a monastic site by groups and individuals, discloses a great deal about the time in which they lived. The picturesque and romantic interpretations, for example, were part of a wider political and social movement. Their preoccupation with ruins in the landscape, seen as part of nature, something to be framed as a picture and described in 'meaningful, comprehensible and differentiated' forms,[2] was the response of a society turning its back on the industrial advances which were changing the world. The scholarly pursuits of antiquarians, archaeologists and historians, in relation to the study of monastic sites, illustrate how these professions were evolving over time and how technology was advancing the knowledge that they were recording.

The incentive for England to 'secure its own heritage against despoliation and decay'[3] was a direct result of these pursuits, and this developed, by the twentieth century, into a determination on the part of the government to conserve the surviving remains. Once ruins became important monuments to be preserved for future generations, interest was encouraged and the rise of mass tourism helped to foster this. Heritage became part of the tourist experience. The packaging and marketing of monastic sites for public consumption has done more than anything to ensure that they are preserved as important historical documents.

All the interpretations of Furness Abbey can be applied to other surviving monastic ruins. All such interpretations are equally valuable to the historian in that they form a part of the history of the site. They also demonstrate how a visual image, such as a ruin, can be viewed in diverse ways which are often influenced by the time in which the interpretation takes place. This study has demonstrated how the monastic ruin has been reclaimed and 'reinvented by the present' in every century from the Dissolution to the present day.[4]

Notes

1. Roth, Lyons and Merewether, *Irresistible Decay*, p. 9.
2. Quote from G. Simmel, in ibid., p. 44.
3. Lowenthal, *Past is a Foreign Country*, pp. xvi–xvii.
4. Lyons, 'Archives in ruins', p. 79.

Bibliography

Printed Primary Sources

A. general works

Axon, E. (ed.), *Bygone Lancashire* (London, 1892).

Ayre, L. R., 'Description of Furness and Furness Abbey from Mrs Radcliffe's "Tour through the English Lake District" ', *The North Lonsdale Magazine and Furness Miscellany*, vols I–II (Ulverston, 1894).

——, 'Notes on Furness Abbey', *The North Lonsdale Magazine and Furness Miscellany* (Ulverston, 1901).

Barnes, F., *Barrow and District: An Illustrated History* (Barrow, 1951).

Beck, T. A., *Annales Furnesienses: History and Antiquities of the Abbey of Furness* (London, 1844).

Binks, G., Dyke, J., and Dagnall, P., *Visitors Welcome: A Manual on the Presentation and Interpretation of Archaeological Excavations* (London, 1988).

Brakspear, H., 'On the first church at Furness', *Trans. of the Lancashire and Cheshire Antiquarian Soc.*, xvii (1900).

Britton, J., *The Beauties of England and Wales; or Original Delineations, Topographical, Historical and Descriptive, of each county*, vol. IX (London, 1807).

Bulmer, J. (ed.), *History, Topography and Directory of Furness and Cartmel comprising its history and archaeology, physical and geological features with separate Historical and Topographical Description of each town, parish and manor* (2nd edn, Preston, 1911).

Carlyle, R., *Six Views of the Ruins of Furness Abbey with a condensed History and Description of the Monastery* (London, 1835).

Cook, E. T., and Wedderburn, A. (eds), *The Works of John Ruskin*, vol. XXXIII (London, 1908).

David, H. H., *A Trip to Furness Abbey and Windermere by a Sentimentalist* (Kirkby Lonsdale, 1845).

Delooze K., and Wood, J., 'Furness Abbey Survey Project: the application of computer graphics and data visualisation to reconstruction modelling of an historic monument', in Lockyear and Rahtz, *Computer Applications and Quantitative Methods*.

Dickinson, J. C., 'Furness Abbey: an archaeological reconsideration', *Trans. of the Cumberland and Westmorland Antiquarian and Archaeological Soc.*, new ser., lxvii (1967).

English Heritage, *The Monuments Protection Programme 1986–96, in retrospect* (London, 1996).

——, *Scheduled Monuments* (London, 1996).

——, *The Monuments Protection Programme: An Introduction* (London, 1997).

——, *Annual Report and Accounts*, 1996/97.

——, 'Transcript of visitors' audio tape' (Furness, 1998).

Farrer, W., and Brownbill, J. (eds), *The Victoria History of the County of Lancaster*, vol. II (London, 1908).

——, *The Victoria History of the Counties of England: A History of Lancashire*, vol. VIII (London, 1914).

Gaythorpe, S. B., 'On the date of the foundation of Furness Abbey', *Trans. Cumberland and Westmorland Antiquarian and Archaeological Soc.*, new ser., xxix (1929).

Gilpin, W., *Observations on the Mountains and Lakes of Cumberland and Westmorland* (London, 1786, repr. Richmond, 1973).

Graham, F., *Picturesque Lancashire* (Newcastle-upon-Tyne, 1969).

Hope, W. H. St John, 'Furness Abbey', *The Builder*, 6 Jul. 1895.

——, 'The Abbey of St Mary in Furness', *Trans. of the Cumberland and Westmorland Antiquarian and Archaeological Soc.*, xvi (1900).

——, *The Abbey of St Mary in Furness* (Kendal, 1902).

Hunt, I. (ed.), *Norman Nicholson's Lakeland: A Prose Anthology* (London, 1991).

Kelly, P. V., 'Dalton Castle', *Trans. Cumberland and Westmorland Antiquarian and Archaeological Soc.*, new ser., xxix (1929).

Kendall, W. B., 'The conventual buildings of the Abbey of Furness', *Barrow Naturalists' Field Club* (Barrow-in-Furness, 1882).

Lockyear, K., and Rahtz, S. (eds), *Computer Applications and Quantitative Methods in Archaeology 1990* (British Archaeological Reports, International Series, No. 565, 1991).

Macaulay, R., *Pleasure of Ruins* (London, 1964).

Mackereth, H. W., *Furness Year Book* (Ulverston, 1900).

Milner, E., and Milner, J. L., *The Churches, Castles and Ancient Halls of North Lancashire*, vol. I (Lancaster, 1880).

Peers, C. R., 'Furness Abbey', *Trans. of the Cumberland and Westmorland Antiquarian Soc.*, new ser., xxix (1929).

Richardson, J., *Furness, Past and Present: Its History and Antiquities*, vols I–II (Barrow-in-Furness, 1880; repr. 1908).

Ruskin, J., *The Seven Lamps of Architecture* (London, 1901).

Stokdyk, J., 'Drawn from the past', *Building*, 30 Aug. 1991.

Walters, J. Cuming, *The Charm of Lancashire* (2nd edn, London, 1930).

Waugh, E., *Waugh's Complete Works: Rambles in the Lake Country*, vol. VII (Manchester, 1882).

West, T., *The Antiquities of Furness* (London, 1774).
——, *The Antiquities of Furness* (Ulverston, 1805).
——, *The Antiquities of Furness* (Ulverston, 1813).
Wood, J., 'Furness Abbey: archaeological work, 1989–1990', *Archaeology North*, i (Jun. 1991).
——, 'Furness Abbey: an integrated and multi-disciplinary approach to the survey, recording, analysis and interpretation of a monastic building', *Religion and Belief*, vi (1992).
——, 'Castles and monasteries', in R. Newman (ed.), *The Archaeology of Lancashire: Present State and Future Priorities* (Lancaster, 1996).
——, 'Record making', *The Building Conservation Directory* (Tisbury, 1996).
Young, A., *A Six Months Tour through the North of England* (London, 1770).
[——], 'Famous Castles and Abbeys', no. xv, 'Furness Abbey', *The Pictorial World*, 18 Jul. 1891.
[——], *History and Directory of Barrow-in-Furness and the whole of North Lonsdale* (publ. Mannex, Preston, 1876).
[——], *History and Directory of Furness and Cartmel* (publ. Mannex, Preston, 1882).

B. guidebooks

Baines, E., *A Companion to the Lakes of Cumberland, Westmorland and Lancashire in a descriptive account of a Family Tour and excursion on horseback and on foot* (2nd edn, London, 1830).
Barber, H., *Shaw's Tourists' Picturesque Guide to Furness Abbey, The Vicinity and Lakes Coniston and Windermere* (8th edn, London, *c.*1878).
Barber, H., *Furness and Cartmel Notes, or Jottings of Topographical, Ecclesiastical and Popular Antiquities, and of Historic Circumstances, as well as Interesting Facts relating to the Districts of Furness and Cartmel* (Ulverston, 1894).
Dickinson, J. C., *Furness Abbey, Lancashire* (first publ. HMSO, London, 1965; repr. 1966, 1970, 1983).
——/English Heritage, *Furness Abbey, Cumbria* (London, 1987; repr. 1989, 1993).
Evans, F., *Furness and Furness Abbey, or a Companion through the Lancashire part of the Lake District* (Ulverston, 1842).
Garton, S. J., *The Ancient Monuments and Historic Buildings: Furness Abbey* (London, 1943, 1945, 1950, 1957).
Harlech, The Rt. Hon. Lord, *Ancient Monuments in the care of the Ministry of Works: Illustrated Regional Guide No. 1: Northern England* (1st edn, 1935; repr. London, 1951).
Harrison, S., Wood, J., and Newman, R./English Heritage, *Furness Abbey, Cumbria* (London, 1998).

Jopling, C. M., *A Sketch of Furness and Cartmel comprising of the Hundred of Lonsdale North of the Sands* (Ulverston, 1843).
Lord, S. S., *Delegates' Guide to Barrow-in-Furness and to the Lake and Sea Trips in the District* (Barrow-in-Furness, 1902).
Martineau, H., *A Description of the English Lakes* (1858, repr. Wakefield, 1974).
Morris, J. P., *A Handy Guide to the Ruins of Furness Abbey*, rev. by J. Turner (Ulverston, *c.* 1855).
[——], *A Guide from Blackpool and Fleetwood to Furness Abbey with a ground plan of the ruins* (Blackpool, 1847).
[——], *A Guide through the Ruins of Furness Abbey with a Brief Account of Dalton and Pile Fouldry* (Ulverston, 1854).
[——], *Handbook to the Abbey of St Mary of Furness in Lancashire* (Ulverston, 1845).
[——], *A Handbook to Furness Abbey: with a Short Account of the Pile of Fouldrey and Rampside to which is appended a condensed description of the Lake District* (Ulverston, *c.*1860).

C. poetry

Wordsworth, W., *The Works of William Wordsworth*, intro. A. Till (Ware, 1994).
[——], *A Pleasure Trip to Furness Abbey by the Steamer the 'Duchess of Lancaster'*, 13 July 1848 (Lancaster, 1895).

D. newspapers

'First Abbey Mass said in 450 years', *Evening Mail*, Friday 21 Sept 1990.

E. miscellaneous

An Illustrated Itinerary of the County of Lancaster (London, 1842).
Order of Service at the Commoration of the 800th Anniversary of the Foundation of Furness Abbey (1927).
Tariff of the Furness Abbey Hotel (Barrow-in-Furness, n.d.).

Secondary Sources

Anderson, M. D., *History and Imagery in British Churches* (London, 1971).
Andrews, M., *The Search for the Picturesque: Landscape Aesthetics and Tourism in Britain, 1760–1800* (Aldershot, 1990).
Ankersmit, F., and Kellner, H. (eds), *A New Philosophy of History* (London, 1995).
Bailey, B., *The National Trust Book of Ruins* (London, 1984).

Bann, S., 'History as competence and performance: notes on the Ironic Museum', in Ankersmit and Kellner, *New Philosophy of History*.

Berkhofer, R. F., 'A point of view on viewpoints in historical practice', in Ankersmit and Kellner, *New Philosophy of History*.

Butler, L., and Given-Wilson, C., *Medieval Monasteries of Great Britain* (London, 1979).

Burkart, A. J., and Medlik, S., *Tourism: Past, Present and Future* (2nd edn, Oxford, 1981).

Chitty, G., 'A prospect of ruins', *Trans. of the Association for Studies in the Conservation of Historic Buildings*, xii (1987).

Clark, K., *The Gothic Revival* (Middlesex, 1962).

Coppack, G., *English Heritage Book of Abbeys and Priories* (London, 1990).

Croall, J., *Preserve or Destroy: Tourism and the Environment* (London, 1995).

Cruickshank, D. (ed.), *Sir Bannister Fletcher's 'A History of Architecture'* (20th edn, London, 1996).

Currie, C. R. J., and Lewis, C. P. (eds), *English County Histories: A Guide* (Stroud, 1994).

Davey, C. R., *Reflections of the Furness Railway* (Barrow, 1984).

Eastaugh, A., and Weiss, N., 'Broadening the market', in Uzzell, *Heritage Interpretation*: vol. II: *Visitor Experience*.

Emerick, K., 'Archaeology and architecture: a tradition of collaboration', *Journal of Architectural Conservation*, i (Mar. 1997).

Emmerson, H., *The Ministry of Works* (London, 1956).

Ewin, A. M., 'Hadrian's Wall: The Social and Cultural History of an Ancient Monument' (Lancaster University, M. A. thesis, 1995).

Fergusson, P., *Architecture of Solitude: Cistercian Abbeys in Twelfth-Century England* (New Jersey, 1984).

Forde, B., *The Pelican Guide to English Literature from Blake to Byron*, vol. V (Middlesex, 1970).

Garrigan, K. O., *Ruskin on Architecture: His Thought and Influence* (Wisconsin, 1973).

Gradon, W. McGowan, *Furness Railway: Its Rise and Development, 1846–1923* (Altrincham, 1946).

Greene, J. P., *Medieval Monasteries* (London, 1995).

Hanley, K., 'Wordsworth's "Region of the Peaceful Self"', in Hanley and Milbank, *From Lancaster to the Lakes*.

——, and Milbank, A. (eds), *From Lancaster to the Lakes: The Region in Literature* (Lancaster, 1992).

Hardy, P. E., *A Guide to the Care and Preservation of Medieval Cathedrals and Churches* (Essex, 1983).

Harris, R. W., *Romanticism and the Social Order, 1780–1830* (London, 1969).

Herbert, D. T. (ed.), *Heritage, Tourism and Society* (London, 1995).

Hewison, R., *Britain in a Climate of Decline* (London, 1987).

Hill, D., *Turner in the North: A Tour through Derbyshire, Yorkshire, Durham,*

Northumberland, The Scottish Borders, The Lake District, Lancashire and Lincolnshire in the year 1797 (New Haven, 1996).
Hughes, M., and Rowley, L. (eds), *The Management and Presentation of Field Monuments* (Oxford, 1986).
Hussy, C., *The Picturesque: Studies in a Point of View* (London, 1967).
Jolley, R., *Edmund Sharpe, 1809–1877: A Lancaster Architect* (Lancaster, 1977).
King, A., *Wordsworth and the Artist's Vision: An Essay in Interpretation* (London, 1966).
Knight, J., *Tintern Abbey and the Romantic Movement* (London, 1977).
Leach, A., *Furness Abbey: A History and Illustrated Guide* (Ulverston, 1988).
Levine, P., *The Amateur and the Professional* (Cambridge, 1986).
Light, D., 'Heritage as informal education', in Herbert, *Heritage, Tourism and Society*.
Lowenthal, D., *The Past is a Foreign Country* (Cambridge, 1985).
Lyons, C., 'Archives in ruins', in Roth, Lyons and Merewether, *Irresistible Decay*.
Melville, J., and Hobbs, J. L., 'Early railway history in Furness', *Trans. of the Cumberland and Westmorland Antiquarian and Archaeological Soc.*, tract ser., xiii (1951).
Merewether, C., 'Traces of loss', in Roth, Lyons and Merewether, *Irresistible Decay*.
Miles, R., *Ann Radcliffe: The Great Enchantress* (Manchester, 1995).
Moir, E., *The Discovery of Britain: The English Tourists, 1540–1840* (London, 1964).
Morris, R., 'Buildings archaeology', in Wood, *Buildings Archaeology*.
Nicholson, N., *The Lakers: The First Tourists* (London, 1972).
Norman, K. J., *Railway Heritage: The Furness Railway. A Recollection* (Peterborough, 1994).
Norton, C., and Park, D. (eds), *Cistercian Art and Architecture in the British Isles* (Cambridge, 1986).
Parkinson, Anne C., *A History of Catholicism in the Furness Peninsula 1127–1997* (Lancaster, 1998).
Pevsner, N., *The Buildings of England. Lancashire 2: The Rural North* (Middlesex, 1969).
Platt, C., *The Abbeys and Priories of Medieval England* (London, 1984).
——, *The Architecture of Medieval Britain* (New Haven, 1990).
Prentice, R., *Tourism and Heritage Attractions* (London, 1993).
Price, J., *Sharpe, Paley and Austin: A Lancaster Architectural Practice, 1836–1942* (Lancaster, 1998).
Quennell, P., *Romantic England: Writing and Painting, 1717–1851* (London, 1970).
Reilly, P., and Rahtz, S. (eds), *Archaeology and the Information Age: A Global Perspective* (London and New York, 1992).
Rodwell, W., *English Heritage Book of Church Archaeology* (London, 1989).

Roth, M. S., Lyons, C., and Merewether, C., *Irresistible Decay: Ruins Reclaimed* (Los Angeles, 1997).

Russell, R., *Discovering Antique Prints* (Aylesbury, 1986).

Salvesen, C., *The Landscape of Memory: A Study of Wordsworth's Poetry* (London, 1965).

Stevenson, J., *British Society, 1914–1945* (London, 1984).

Thompson, M. W., *Ruins: Their Preservation and Display* (London, 1981).

Urry, J., *The Tourist Gaze: Leisure and Travel in Contemporary Societies* (London, 1990).

Uzzell, D. L. (ed.), *Heritage Interpretation*, vol. II: *The Visitor Experience* (London, 1989).

Walton, J., *Dalton-in-Furness: A Concise History* (Dalton, 1972).

Walton, J. K., and McGloin, P. R., 'The tourist trade in Victorian Lakeland', *Northern History*, xvii (1981).

Watson, J. R., *Picturesque Landscape and English Romantic Poetry* (London, 1970).

Wilson, C., 'The Cistercians as "Missionaries of the Gothic" in Northern England', in Norton and Park, *Cistercian Art and Architecture*.

Wood, J. (ed.), *Buildings Archaeology: Applications in Practice* (Oxford, 1994).

——, and Chapman, G., 'Three-dimensional computer visualization of historic buildings: with particular reference to reconstruction modelling', in Reilly and Rahtz, *Archaeology and the Information Age*.

Wright, P., *On Living in an Old Country* (London, 1985).

Index

NB Numbers in *italics*, following text references, are figure numbers.